Barbara Clemens

MT Cozzola

Barbara Waxer

upgrading to
Microsoft® Office 2010

COURSE TECHNOLOGY
CENGAGE Learning

Australia • Brazil • Japan • Korea • Mexico • Singapore • Spain • United Kingdom • United States

COURSE TECHNOLOGY
CENGAGE Learning™

Upgrading to Microsoft® Office 2010
Clemens/Cozzola/Waxer

Vice President, Publisher: Nicole J. Pinard

Executive Editor: Marjorie Hunt

Executive Editor, SAM: Damaris Curran Herlihy

Senior Editor, SAM: Amanda Shelton

Associate Acquisitions Editor: Brandi Shailer

Senior Product Manager: Christina Kling Garrett

Technology Product Manager: Jan Immerman

Associate Product Manager: Michelle Camisa

Editorial Assistant: Kim Klasner

Director of Marketing: Cheryl Costantini

Senior Marketing Manager: Ryan DeGrote

Senior Technology Marketing Manager:
    Kristin Taggart

Marketing Coordinator: Kristen Panciocco

Contributing Author: Lisa Ruffolo

Developmental Editors: Barbara Clemens,
    MT Cozzola, Lisa Ruffolo, Barbara Waxer

Content Project Manager: Heather Hopkins

Copy Editor: Mark Goodin

Proofreader: Harold Johnson

Indexer: Rich Carlson

Print Buyer: Fola Orekoya

QA Manuscript Reviewers: John Frietas,
    Serge Palladino, Jeff Schwartz, Marianne Snow,
    Susan Whalen

Cover Designer: GEX Publishing Services

Composition: GEX Publishing Services

For product information and technology assistance, contact us at
Cengage Learning Customer & Sales Support, 1-800-354-9706
For permission to use material from this text or product, submit all
requests online at **www.cengage.com/permissions**
Further permissions questions can be emailed to
permissionrequest@cengage.com

Library of Congress Control Number: 2010925891

ISBN-13: 978-0-538-47288-3

ISBN-10: 0-538-47288-X

Course Technology
20 Channel Center Street
Boston, MA 02210
USA

Cengage Learning is a leading provider of customized learning solutions with office locations around the globe, including Singapore, the United Kingdom, Australia, Mexico, Brazil, and Japan. Locate your local office at:
international.cengage.com/region

Cengage Learning products are represented in Canada by Nelson Education, Ltd.

To learn more about Course Technology, visit **www.cengage.com/coursetechnology**

To learn more about Cengage Learning, visit **www.cengage.com**

Purchase any of our products at your local college store or at our preferred online store
www.cengagebrain.com

Printed in the United States of America
1 2 3 4 5 6 7 8 9 18 17 16 15 14 13 12 11 10

Brief Contents

Contents

Access 2010

PowerPoint 2010

Web Apps 2010

About This Book

Welcome to *Upgrading to Microsoft Office 2010*!

This book is designed to help you learn all the exciting new features of Microsoft Office 2010! This book is for you if:

- you already know Microsoft Office 2007 and just want to learn the new features of Microsoft Office 2010
- you are learning Microsoft Office 2007 now, but want to be ready to move to Office 2010 when you get the new software

This book is designed to make it easy to find information. Each chapter focuses on one of the four major programs in Microsoft Office and covers the key new features of each. The chapters are organized by lessons, which are presented on two-facing pages, making it easy to see what's new at a glance.

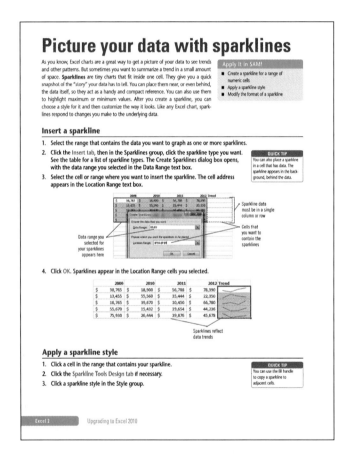

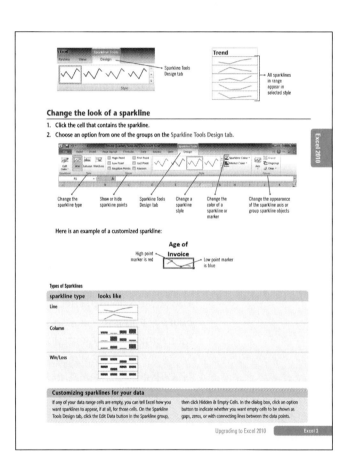

Using this book with SAM 2007 v6.0

You can try out many of the new features covered in this book in SAM v6.0, which includes nearly 100 simulated tasks on Microsoft Office 2010 that give you hands-on experience with the new features of the software. Look for the SAM task reference table at the beginning of each chapter for a list of SAM tasks covered. Most lessons also include an Apply it in SAM! box that list SAM tasks related to the lesson. The Getting Started with SAM chapter provides instructions for how to use SAM.

Apply It in SAM!

- Create a sparkline for a range of numeric cells
- Apply a sparkline style
- Modify the format of a sparkline

About SAM

SAM is the premier proficiency-based assessment and training environment for Microsoft Office. Web-based software along with an inviting user interface provide maximum teaching and learning flexibility. SAM builds students' skills and confidence with a variety of real-life simulations, and SAM Projects' assignments prepare students for today's workplace.

The SAM system includes Assessment, Training, and Projects, featuring page references and remediation for Course Technology's Microsoft Office textbooks. With SAM, instructors can enjoy the flexibility of creating assignments based on content from their favorite Microsoft Office books or based on specific course objectives. Instructors appreciate the scheduling and reporting options that have made SAM the market-leading online testing and training software for over a decade. Over 2,000 performance-based questions and matching Training simulations, as well as tens of thousands of objective-based questions from many Course Technology texts, provide instructors with a variety of choices across multiple applications from the introductory level through the comprehensive level. The inclusion of hands-on Projects guarantee that student knowledge will skyrocket from the practice of solving real-world situations using Microsoft Office software.

SAM Assessment
- Content for these hands-on, performance-based tasks includes Word, Excel, Access, PowerPoint, Internet Explorer, Outlook, and Windows. Includes tens of thousands of objective-based questions from many Course Technology texts.

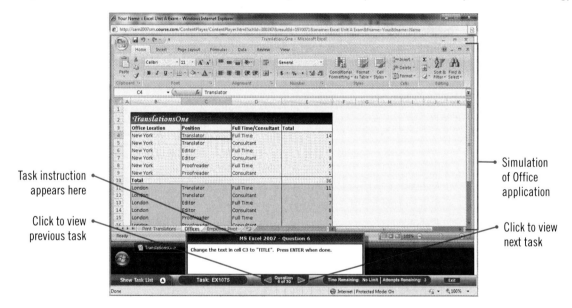

Task instruction appears here

Click to view previous task

Simulation of Office application

Click to view next task

SAM Training
- Observe mode allows the student to watch and listen to a task as it is being completed.
- Practice mode allows the student to follow guided arrows and hear audio prompts to help visual learners know how to complete a task.
- Apply mode allows the student to prove what they've learned by completing a task using helpful instructions.

SAM Projects
- Live-in-the-application assignments in Word, Excel, Access and PowerPoint that help students be sure they know how to effectively communicate, solve a problem or make a decision.
- Students receive detailed feedback on their project within minutes.
- Additionally, teaches proper file management techniques.
- Ensures that academic integrity is not compromised, with unique anti-cheating detection encrypted into the data files.

Microsoft Office 2010 Tasks Covered in SAM 2007 v6.0

Word

- Start Word
- Create a new blank document
- Use Word Help
- Open an existing document
- Print a document
- Find and replace text
- Save a document with a new filename
- Save a document
- Customize the Quick Access Toolbar
- Zoom in on a document
- Insert a SmartArt graphic
- Modify a SmartArt graphic
- Remove the background of a picture
- Modify the tone of a picture
- Recolor a picture
- Increase the sharpness of a picture
- Decrease the sharpness of a pictures
- Insert a screenshot
- Search for text
- Exit Word

Excel

- Start Excel
- Locate and open an existing workbook
- Print a worksheet
- Save a file to a different location
- Save a workbook with a new name
- Save to SkyDrive
- Customize the Quick Access Toolbar
- Zoom in on a worksheet
- Apply conditional formatting to a range of cells
- Create a sparkline for a range of numeric cells
- Apply a sparkline style
- Modify the format of a sparkline
- Edit a conditional formatting rule
- Check a workbook's accessibility
- Add alternate text to a chart
- Customize the Ribbon
- In a PivotTable, insert a slicer for one category
- Use the slicer to display the PivotTable data for a category
- Cancel a filter
- Delete the slicer
- Edit data in an online worksheet
- Close a worksheet and exit Excel

Access

- Start Access
- Create a new blank database
- Open a database
- Create a table in Datasheet view
- Create a table in Design view
- Change the data type of a field in Datasheet view
- Define number and currency fields in a table
- Create a query using the Simple Query Wizard
- Add a calculated field to a query
- Create a table from an application part
- Change a data type in Design view
- Change a data type in Datasheet view
- Create a form using the Form Wizard
- Create a new form in Design view
- Create a report using the Report Wizard
- Create a report in Design view
- Print a report
- Delete a database object
- Rename a database object
- Copy a database object
- Group objects
- Create a macro
- Undo current changes
- Compact a database
- Use the Backup Database command

PowerPoint

- Start PowerPoint
- Close a presentation
- Create a new presentation from a template
- Open an existing presentation
- Use PowerPoint Help
- Print speaker notes
- Save a presentation
- Apply transition effects to a single slide
- Undo an action
- Zoom in on a slide
- Apply an entrance animation effect to a shape
- Insert a SmartArt graphic
- Animate a shape using a motion path
- Use the Animation Painter
- Apply an effect to a video
- Apply an effect to an image
- Format an image
- Insert a section into a slide show
- Insert video in a slide
- Trim an inserted video
- Add a trigger to media
- Broadcast a slide show
- Record a slide show as a video
- Compress media
- Exit PowerPoint

Getting Started with SAM

SAM 2007 is a powerful software that helps you learn Microsoft Office 2007—and now, with SAM 2007 v6.0 you can experience Microsoft Office 2010, too. There are three main components in SAM. **SAM Assessment** simulates Office applications, allowing you to demonstrate your computer knowledge in a hands-on environment. **SAM Training** helps you learn in the way that works best for you: observe how an Office skill is performed, or practice and apply what you've learned. **SAM Projects** lets you work live-in-the-application on project-based assignments so that you can understand how applications can help you be successful in the business world.

SAM 2007 v6.0 includes Assessment and Training simulations based on features new to Office 2010, almost all of which are referenced in this book. If your school has not upgraded to Microsoft Office 2010, you can get a first look at the new features of Office 2010 by reviewing the chapters in this text. Then, your instructor may assign a SAM Exam or Training that includes these Office 2010 simulations. ■ This chapter provides basic instruction on how to get started using SAM 2007 using Assessment and Training in SAM 2007.

How do I know what features of Office 2010 are covered in SAM?

You can find references to SAM throughout the book. Each chapter starts with a SAM reference table that lists the SAM Assessment and Training simulations covered in the chapter. As you go through the chapter, look for the Apply it in SAM! boxes in most lessons that list the SAM simulations that relate to the lesson.

Lessons

Log in to SAM 2007

Join a section and view assignments

Use SAM Training

Take a SAM Exam

View SAM Exam results

Log in to SAM 2007

To log in and use SAM, you must have a SAM 2007 username and password. If your school has preregistered you as a SAM user, then your instructor will provide you with a username and password that you can use to log in on the SAM 2007 log in page. If your school has not preregistered you as a SAM user, you will need to create a SAM user profile for yourself. **NOTE**: *To set up a SAM user profile, you must have an Institution Key, which your instructor will provide to you.* Follow the appropriate instructions below to log in to SAM.

Log in to SAM if you are a preregistered SAM user

1. **Be sure you are connected to the Internet, start Internet Explorer or Firefox, type** http://sam2007.course.com **in the Address bar, then press [Enter]. The SAM login page opens.**

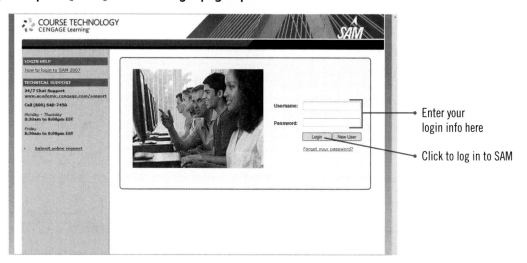

Enter your login info here

Click to log in to SAM

2. **Type your username and password, then click Login. The SAM Welcome page opens.**

Log in to SAM if you are *not* a preregistered SAM user

1. Be sure you are connected to the Internet, start Internet Explorer or Firefox, type http://sam2007.course.com in the Address bar, then press [Enter].

2. Click New user. Type your school's Institution Key in the Institution Key field, then click Submit.

> **QUICK TIP**
> An Institution Key is an 8-digit code that uniquely identifies your school. Your instructor will provide you with your school's Institution Key, which is in this format: V7xxxxxx.

Type your school's Institution Key here

3. In the dialog box that opens, verify that the Institution Key matches the one for your school, then click OK.

> **TROUBLE**
> If your institution is using the key code version of SAM 2007, a page opens after Step 3 that requests your 18-digit key code. You can find this key code inside the flap of the SAM 2007 card you received when you purchased your textbook(s). Enter the key code exactly as printed.

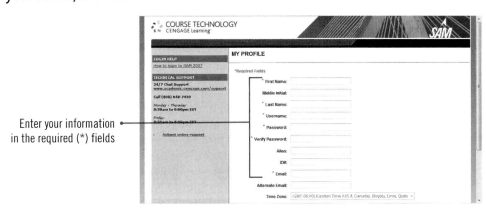

Enter your information in the required (*) fields

4. Enter your information in all of the required (*) fields, including a secret question and answer that will be used for security purposes should you ever forget your password.

5. Click Save.

6. Verify that all of the information on the user profile page is accurate, then click Confirm. The Terms & Conditions page opens.

7. Read the terms of the SAM 2007 TERMS and CONDITIONS agreement, then click I Agree. The SAM Welcome page opens.

Join a section and view assignments

To take any SAM assignments, you must first join a section (or a class). Once you have joined, then you will be able to access and complete specific SAM assignments that your instructor has assigned.

Join a Section

1. **Click** Sections **in the left Navigation Pane.**

2. **Click** Join a Section **in the upper-right corner. The My Sections page now displays all the sections that are available for you to join.**

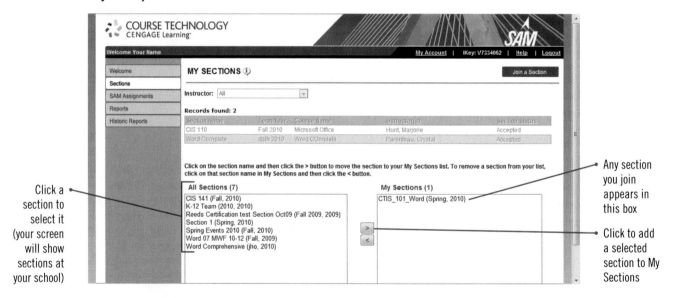

3. **Click the section listed in the All Sections box that you want to join, then click the** right arrow button **next to the All Sections box. If you make a mistake, click the** left arrow button **to remove a section.**
4. **Click** Save, **then click** OK **in the dialog box that opens, if necessary. Now you can access the assignments scheduled for the section you joined.**

View SAM assignments

1. Click SAM Assignments in the left Navigation Pane to open the My SAM Assignments page. The SAM exams or training assignments for your section are listed.

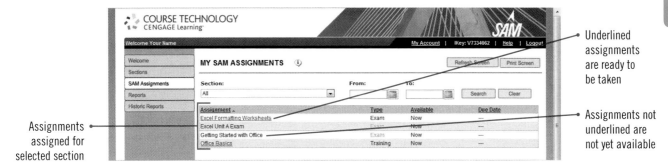

Underlined assignments are ready to be taken

Assignments not underlined are not yet available

Assignments assigned for selected section

2. Click an assignment in the list. An Assignment Details window opens.

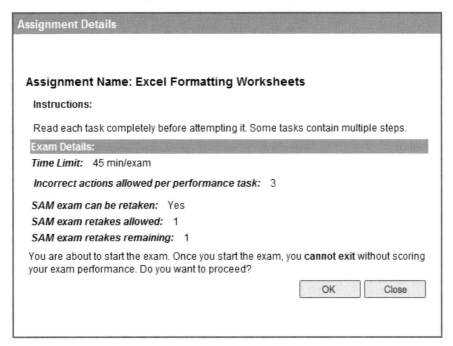

3. Click OK to launch the specific SAM assignment. Read more about exam and training assignments in the next two sections.

Use SAM Training

Once you have joined a section, you can complete any SAM Training assignments that appear on the My SAM Assignments page, as assigned by your instructor. SAM Training provides hands-on simulations to help you learn in the way that works best for you. SAM Training has three training modes to best suit your style. **Observe mode** lets you watch and listen as steps for the task are completed and explained on-screen in a movie medium. **Practice mode** lets you complete steps one at a time, guided by the voice of a narrator and on-screen callouts. **Apply mode** lets you try the task more independently with only the task instruction on-screen. Once you complete a learning mode for one task, you click the Task Complete button to move to the next mode or the next task, if all modes are complete for that task. SAM Training modes can be completed in any order. However, you must click Task Complete after the Apply method to receive credit (a check mark) for that skill. This lesson provides instructions for using all three training modes.

Complete a training task in observe mode

1. On the My SAM Assignments page, click a SAM training assignment. A Task Assignment Details window opens.
2. Click OK. The SAM Player launches and displays a description of the first training task.

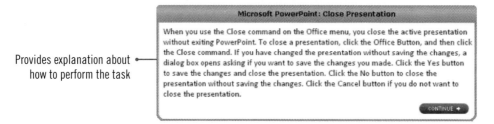

Provides explanation about how to perform the task

3. Click Continue to launch the training task in Observe Mode.
4. Watch and listen to the animation until a window appears that says you have completed the task.
5. Click Task Complete to advance the training task to Practice mode.

Complete a training task in practice mode

1. Click the Practice button on the SAM Player, then click Continue.
2. Complete each step as directed.
3. Click Task Complete when you have completed all the steps.

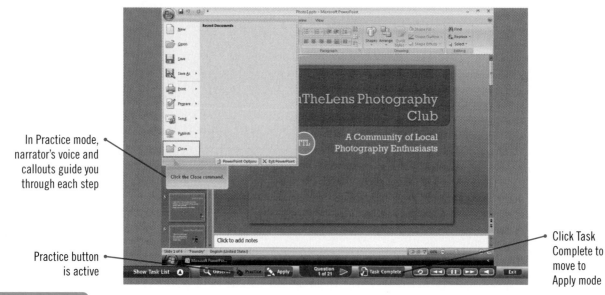

In Practice mode, narrator's voice and callouts guide you through each step

Practice button is active

Click Task Complete to move to Apply mode

Complete a training task in apply mode

1. Click the Apply button on the SAM Player, then click Continue.
2. Read the instructions and complete the steps.
3. Click Task Complete when you have completed all the steps. Doing so will ensure that you receive a check mark in the Task List. This is only necessary for the Apply mode.

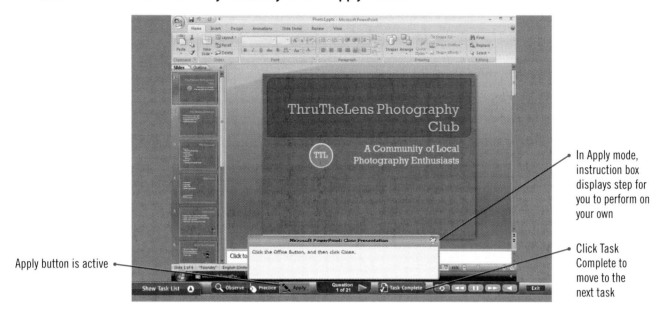

Apply button is active

In Apply mode, instruction box displays step for you to perform on your own

Click Task Complete to move to the next task

Take a SAM Exam

Once you have joined a section, you can take a SAM Exam. When an instructor creates an Exam, he or she may schedule it for a certain time period, so make sure you know when the Exam is available. Your instructor might also specify a password to access the exam, so make sure you know what it is. After taking a SAM Exam, you can view your results in the Reports area, if your instructor has made that option available to you.

Start a SAM Exam

1. Click SAM Assignments in the SAM navigation bar. My SAM Assignments page opens.
2. Click the Exam you want to complete in the Assignment column. (*Note:* If a Password Details dialog box opens, type the instructor-provided password then click OK.) The Assignment Details dialog box opens.
3. Read the Assignment Details dialog box, then click OK. The SAM Player launches, as shown below.

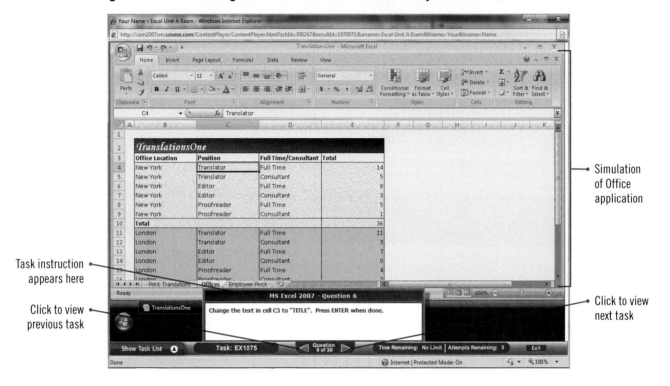

Simulation of Office application

Task instruction appears here

Click to view previous task

Click to view next task

Perform a SAM Exam task

1. Read the task in the Questions Area, then use your skills to perform the task.
2. If you complete the task correctly, the window below briefly appears and the next task appears in the Questions Area.

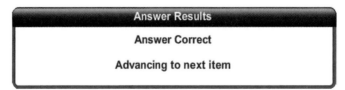

3. If you complete the task incorrectly, this window appears.

4. To try the task again, click Retry; to skip the task click Go to the next task. *Note*: You can only retry a task if your instructor has set up SAM to allow multiple attempts.

Use the Task List to move to a specific task

1. Click the Show Task List button.

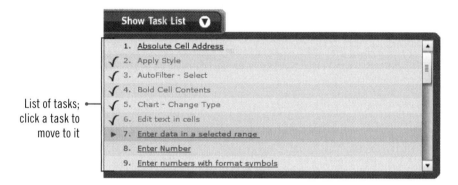

List of tasks; click a task to move to it

2. Click the task you want to move to.
3. Click the Show Task List button to close the Task List.

View SAM Exam results

When you complete a SAM Exam, you can view your results to see your grade. Your instructor might specify that SAM display your results to you right after you take the exam, in which case the results will appear after you complete all the tasks for an exam. Your instructor might also specify that results will be available through Reports at some later time. You can also view the results of any SAM Training tasks you have completed.

View your Exam results

1. Click Reports in the Navigation Pane to view the My Reports page.

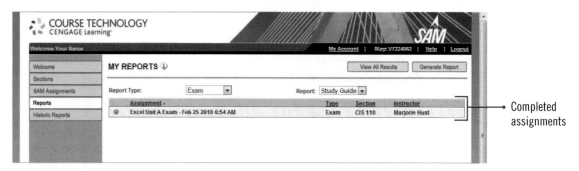

Completed assignments

2. Click the assignment you want to see a report for.
3. Click the Report Type list arrow, then click the appropriate option (Exam, Training, or Project).
4. Click the Report list arrow, then click Study Guide.
5. Click the Generate Report button to view the report.

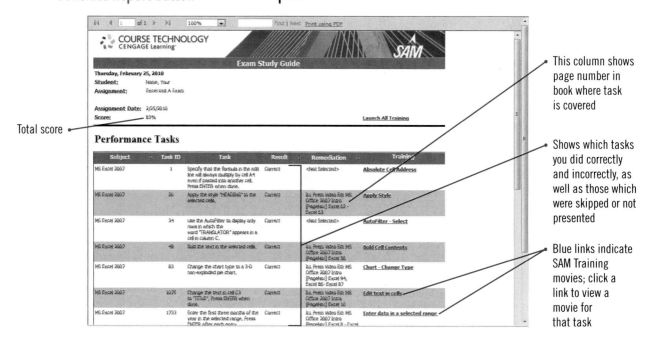

This column shows page number in book where task is covered

Total score

Shows which tasks you did correctly and incorrectly, as well as those which were skipped or not presented

Blue links indicate SAM Training movies; click a link to view a movie for that task

Getting Started with SAM

Upgrading to Word 2010

Word 2010 introduces new features, enhancements to familiar tools, and a more integrated user interface. Commands and options are arranged to take better advantage of screen real estate, to lay out commands and options, and to integrate more options and commands. Word 2007 users will recognize the familiar Ribbon interface, but you will also notice some important changes, including the absence of the Office button and the introduction of the File tab. Once you begin working with the new structure, you'll see how many items are now logically pulled together in one place for related tasks. Fans of keyboard shortcuts will find that most shortcuts from previous versions of Word work just fine, so transitioning is a breeze. ■■·■ As you review these lessons, you will be able to practice many of the skills using Skills Assessment Manager (SAM). The lessons will cover SAM skills and tasks as outlined in this table:

Lesson	SAM Tasks
Open, create, and print in Backstage view	■ Open an existing document ■ Create a new, blank document ■ Print a document ■ Exit Word
Save and send in Backstage view	■ Save a document ■ Save a document with a new filename
Search and navigate a document	■ Search for text
Add pictures to your SmartArt	■ Insert a SmartArt Graphic ■ Modify a SmartArt Graphic
Get creative with picture tools	■ Modify the tone of a picture ■ Recolor a picture ■ Increase the sharpness of a picture ■ Decrease the sharpness of a picture
Tap into more powerful graphics	■ Remove the background of a picture ■ Insert a screen capture of the current window ■ Take a custom screen clipping
Explore other Word improvements	■ Use Word Help
Other Lessons	
Translate text and documents	

Open, print, and create in Backstage view

One of the first things you'll notice in Word 2010 is the new **File tab** on the Ribbon. Click it to open **Backstage view**, which brings together all your file-related tasks and program options. This is the place to go to open, create, and save documents; change options; exit the program; and much more. In place of the Office button from Word 2007 is the Word program icon. You can use it to resize, move, or close the program window.

Open an existing document

1. **Click the File tab on the Ribbon to open Backstage view. If a document is currently open, the Info tab is in front.**

   File tab →

2. **Choose how to open your document.**

   To open the Open dialog box, click here

   Info tab is in front

   To choose from a list of recently opened documents, click here

   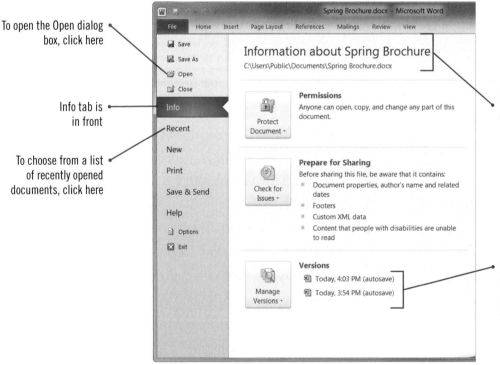

   Name and file path of currently open document

   To open an earlier version of the current document, click a document listed here, then save it under a new name

Create a new document

1. Click the File tab on the Ribbon to open Backstage view, then click New on the Navigation bar.

2. Click any category to see the templates available in the center pane. When browsing for a template, click the Home button 🏠 to return to to the main pane, or use the Back button ⬅ and Forward button ➡ to navigate.

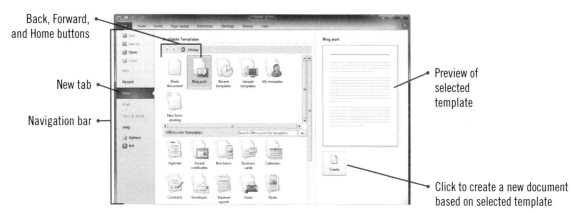

Back, Forward, and Home buttons

New tab

Navigation bar

Preview of selected template

Click to create a new document based on selected template

3. When you find the template you want, click Create; or, if the template is located on Office.com, click Download. A new document based on the template opens.

Preview and print a document

1. Click the File tab on the Ribbon, then click Print on the Navigation bar.

2. Adjust the settings in the center pane the way you want them.

QUICK TIP

To exit Word, click the File tab on the Ribbon, then click Exit on the Navigation bar. You will be prompted to close any open documents.

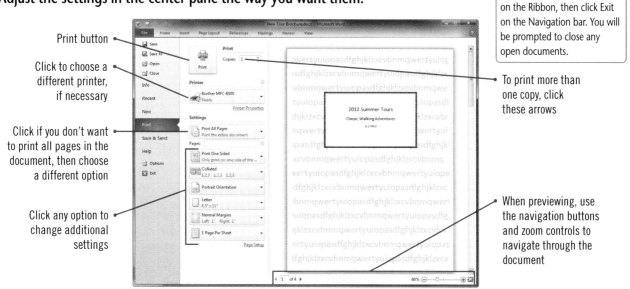

Print button

Click to choose a different printer, if necessary

Click if you don't want to print all pages in the document, then choose a different option

Click any option to change additional settings

To print more than one copy, click these arrows

When previewing, use the navigation buttons and zoom controls to navigate through the document

3. When you're ready, click Print.

Working in Protected view

If you open a document from a source that Word considers risky, such as a document you've downloaded from the Internet or received as an e-mail attachment, the document opens in Protected view, to protect your computer against any malicious code that might be contained in the file. **Protected view** allows you to read, but not edit the document. If you're not certain of the document's origin, stay in Protected mode to view the document. To get more information about the file, such as the author or creation date, switch to Backstage view and review the information on the Info page. If you're confident the file is from a trustworthy source, you can access all your editing features by clicking the Enable Editing button in the red warning bar across the top of the document window.

Save and send in Backstage view

The basic process of saving a Word document hasn't changed much in Word 2010; you access the Save and Save As commands on the Navigation bar in Backstage view, but beyond that, things look familiar. What has changed is how much easier it is to access other ways of storing and distributing your documents. Backstage view makes it easier to e-mail a document, save it to a shared location like your SkyDrive, publish it as a blog post, quickly create a PDF or XPS file, and much more.

Save a document using a new name or location

1. Click the File tab on the Ribbon to open Backstage view, then click Save As on the Navigation bar. The Save As dialog box opens.

2. Choose the options you want.

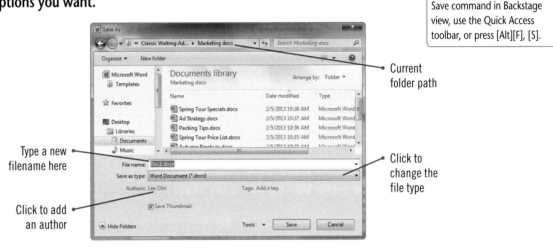

Current folder path

Type a new filename here

Click to change the file type

Click to add an author

3. When you're finished, click Save.

Save a document to your SkyDrive

1. Click the File tab on the Ribbon, then click Save & Send on the Navigation bar.

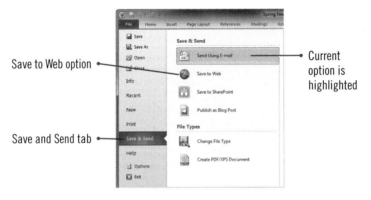

Save to Web option

Current option is highlighted

Save and Send tab

2. Click Save to Web.

3. If you are not currently signed into Windows Live, click the Sign in button 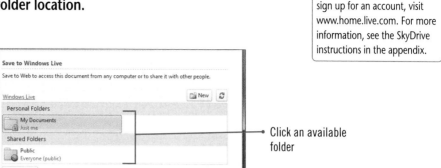. Type your username and password in the Windows Security dialog box, then click OK.

4. Under Windows Live, choose a folder location.

Click an available folder

Click to open Save As dialog box

5. Click the Save as button . The Save as dialog box opens, with the folder location showing the file path you specified in the previous step. Select the options you want, then click OK.

Send a document using e-mail

1. Click the File tab on the Ribbon to open Backstage view, then click Save & Send on the Navigation bar.

2. Click Send Using E-mail in the center pane. Under Send Using E-mail, click an option to indicate how you want to send this file.

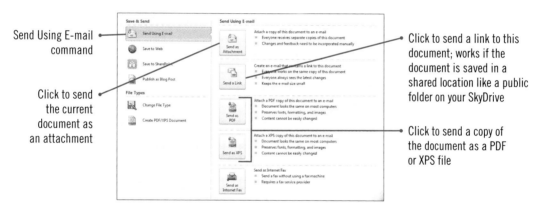

Send Using E-mail command

Click to send the current document as an attachment

Click to send a link to this document; works if the document is saved in a shared location like a public folder on your SkyDrive

Click to send a copy of the document as a PDF or XPS file

Here, we've clicked Send as an Attachment, so you see the name of the file in the Attached line.

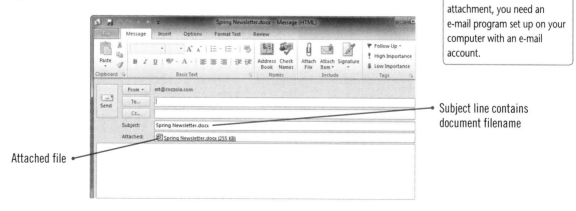

Subject line contains document filename

Attached file

3. Complete the e-mail message, then click Send.

Search and navigate a document

The Navigation pane in Word 2010 offers a whole new way to interact with your documents. If you used the Document Map or Thumbnails pane in Word 2007 you'll find this feature is much more powerful and flexible. It provides a thumbnail view of all the pages, sections, or search results within an entire document, which is especially helpful if you work with long documents. You can use this pane to search for text, pictures, and other elements, and to rearrange sections by heading. The pane is easy to move and resize, so you might want to leave it open as you work, even if you're not currently searching for something.

Apply It in SAM!

■ Search for text

Display, move, or hide the Navigation pane

1. Click the View tab on the Ribbon.
2. Click the Navigation Pane check box in the Show group to select it, if necessary. The Navigation pane opens.

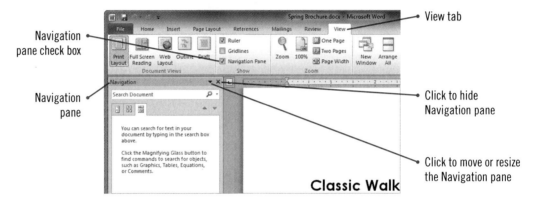

Navigation pane check box

Navigation pane

View tab

Click to hide Navigation pane

Click to move or resize the Navigation pane

Classic Walk

3. If you want to move the pane, click the Navigation pane list arrow, then click Move; or simply point to the top of the Navigation pane. The mouse pointer changes to a move pointer ⊕, which you can drag to move the pane. Double-click the top of the pane to re-dock it.
4. If the pane is too large or too small, click the Navigation pane list arrow, then click Size, or simply point to the right edge of the task pane. The mouse pointer changes to a resizing arrow ↔, which you can use to adjust the width of the pane.

Search for text

1. Click the Home tab on the Ribbon, then click Find in the Editing group.
2. In the Search Document text box, start typing the word or phrase you want to find. In the Navigation pane, Word immediately lists all matches, and the matches are also highlighted in the document.

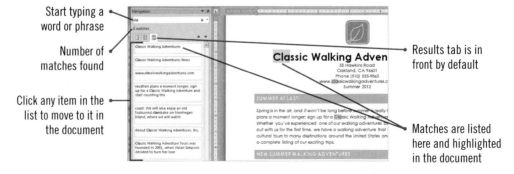

Start typing a word or phrase

Number of matches found

Click any item in the list to move to it in the document

Results tab is in front by default

Matches are listed here and highlighted in the document

3. Click any match in the Results tab to move to that item in the document. Use a different tab in the Navigation pane to navigate based on headings or pages instead of results:

- Click the Pages tab, and all pages that contain at least one match are highlighted. Click any page to move to it.
- Click the Headings tab, and all headings that contain at least one match are highlighted. Click any item in the pane to move to that location.

4. To replace the matched text with something else, click the Search Options button 🔍, then click Replace (or, click the Replace button in the Editing group on the Home tab).

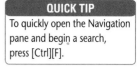

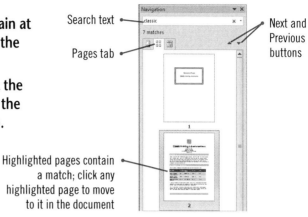

Search text •
Pages tab •
Next and Previous buttons •

Highlighted pages contain a match; click any highlighted page to move to it in the document

Search for graphics, tables, and other elements

1. In the Navigation pane, click the Magnifying Glass list arrow 🔍 ▾. In the menu that opens, click the element you want to search for.

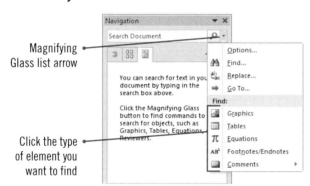

Magnifying Glass list arrow •

Click the type of element you want to find •

2. Click the Next Search Result button ▼ and Previous Search Result button ▲ to jump to each match in the document.

3. When you find the object you need, just click in the document and the items are no longer highlighted. Click the Close button ✖, and the search is cleared.

Navigate and rearrange headings

1. To browse through a document that contains headings, click the Headings tab in the Navigation pane.

2. Click any heading to move to that part of the document. To rearrange the headings, simply drag them up or down in the list.

3. To browse through the pages of a multipage document, click the Pages tab. Click any page icon to move to that page. (*Note*: You cannot rearrange pages using the Navigation pane.)

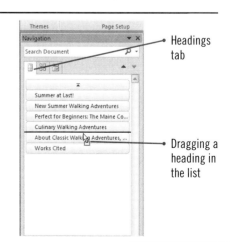

Headings tab •

Dragging a heading in the list •

Add pictures to your SmartArt

Word 2010 offers dozens of new SmartArt layouts, including a brand-new category, Pictures. With Picture layouts, you use your own picture files as part of the design. Once you've created a SmartArt graphic using a Picture layout, modifying the pictures is just as easy as changing the text.

Insert a SmartArt graphic

1. Click in the document where you want to insert a SmartArt graphic.
2. Click the Insert tab on the Ribbon, then click SmartArt in the Illustrations group.

> **QUICK TIP**
> The Picture category pulls together all picture layouts that are available in other categories, such as List and Relationship.

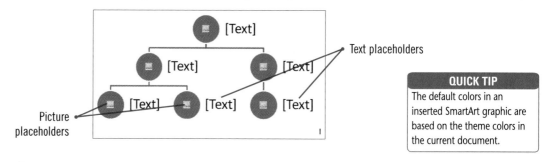

Click a category

Click a layout

Preview the selected layout

Click to insert the selected layout

3. Make your selections, then click OK. The new graphic is inserted in your document. Picture SmartArt graphics containing pictures include text placeholders and picture placeholders.

Text placeholders

Picture placeholders

> **QUICK TIP**
> The default colors in an inserted SmartArt graphic are based on the theme colors in the current document.

Add pictures and text to a SmartArt graphic

1. Click a picture placeholder in the SmartArt graphic.
2. Locate the picture you want to insert in the Insert Picture dialog box.

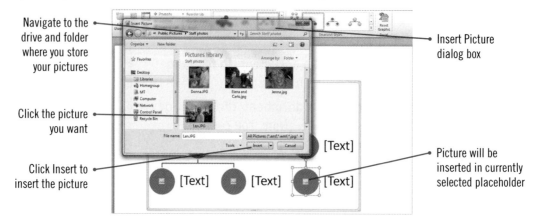

Navigate to the drive and folder where you store your pictures

Click the picture you want

Click Insert to insert the picture

Insert Picture dialog box

Picture will be inserted in currently selected placeholder

3. Click a text placeholder, then type your text.

4. Click outside the picture and text to deselect them. Word not only sizes the text to fit, it crops and sizes your picture file to fit into the SmartArt picture shape.

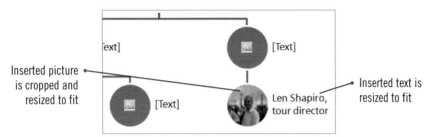

Inserted picture is cropped and resized to fit

Inserted text is resized to fit

Len Shapiro, tour director

Change a picture in a SmartArt graphic

1. Double-click the picture you want to change in the SmartArt graphic. The picture is selected, and the SmartArt Tools and Picture Tools tabs become available.

2. Click the Picture Tools Format tab to modify all aspects of the picture within the SmartArt graphic.

Use tools on this tab to adjust the selected picture within the SmartArt graphic

Crop tool currently selected

Click to replace the selected picture with a different picture

Drag to resize the picture within the shape

3. Click the SmartArt Tools Design tab and the SmartArt Tools Format tab to make changes to the SmartArt shape.

Changing the shape of the selected element

Use SmartArt Tools tabs to adjust the graphic and elements within it

QUICK TIP

If you don't like the changes you make to a shape, select it and then click the Reset Graphic button on the SmartArt Tools Design tab.

4. When you're finished, click outside the diagram to deselect it.

Adding alt text to pictures

If you plan to distribute a document electronically, especially one that people may read using a Web browser, you may want to add alt text to your pictures and tables. **Alt text** is text that describes a graphic element for people who may not be able to see or interpret the element, due to a disability or the type of device they're using to read your document. By including alt text, you create a more universally accessible document and a more complete communication experience. To add alt text to a picture, table, graph, or other inserted object, right-click the selected object, then in the shortcut menu click Format Picture. The Format Picture dialog box opens. (You can also open this dialog box by clicking the dialog launcher in the Picture Styles group on the Picture Tools Format tab.) In the dialog box, click the Alt Text tab, type a title for the object in the Title text box, a more detailed description in the Description text box, then click Close. Remember that people will use this text to understand what the object shows, so be as detailed as possible while keeping the message concise and to the point.

Get creative with picture tools

The Picture Tools Format tab features new and improved tools for improving the look of any picture. In Office 2010, you can adjust color saturation and tone, using presets or exact settings, and recolor using the exact shade you want. You can also preview all of these effects much more immediately than before, because the selected picture is integrated into the tool galleries. You can apply all sorts of effects to a picture, like a pencil sketch, an oil painting, or glowing edges, all with just one click on the Artistic Effects gallery.

Change a picture's color and tone

1. Click an inserted picture to select it, click the Picture Tools Format tab on the Ribbon, then click Color in the Adjust group. The Color gallery displays preset Color Saturation, Color Tone, and Recolor options, using the selected image for a preview.

2. Under each category, point to any option to preview the effect in the document. You might want to scroll in your document so that you can easily see the picture with the palette open.

> **QUICK TIP**
>
> To access commonly used picture tools without using the Ribbon, right-click a picture; the Mini toolbar displays tools relevant to the current selection, such as Crop and Rotate.

Color button

The current setting in each category is highlighted

Click to open Picture Color Options dialog box, where you can make more precise adjustments

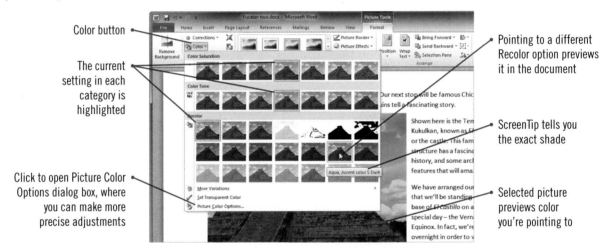

Pointing to a different Recolor option previews it in the document

ScreenTip tells you the exact shade

Selected picture previews color you're pointing to

3. Click any option to select it, then reopen the gallery to make additional changes.

Make picture corrections

1. With a picture selected, click Corrections in the Adjust group on the Picture Tools Format tab.

2. To sharpen the picture, click an option to the right of the current settings. To soften the picture, click an option to the left of the current setting.

3. To increase brightness, choose an option to the right of the current selection; to decrease it, choose an option to the left.

4. To increase contrast, choose an option below the current choice; to decrease it, choose an option above the current selection.

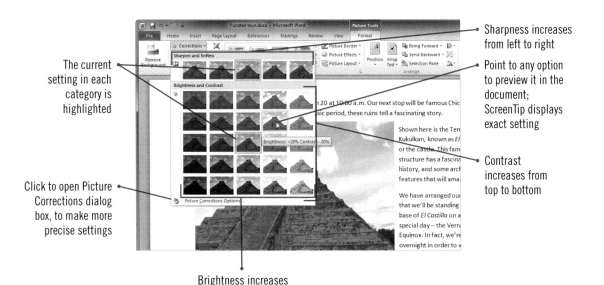

The current setting in each category is highlighted

Sharpness increases from left to right

Point to any option to preview it in the document; ScreenTip displays exact setting

Contrast increases from top to bottom

Click to open Picture Corrections dialog box, to make more precise settings

Brightness increases from left to right

Apply artistic effects

1. With a picture selected, click Artistic Effects in the Adjust group on the Picture Tools Format tab. The Artistic Effects gallery opens.

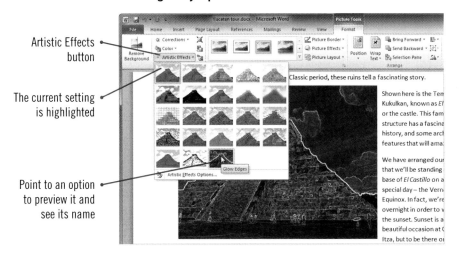

Artistic Effects button

The current setting is highlighted

Point to an option to preview it and see its name

2. Click an effect to apply it to the picture.

Applying a Picture Layout

The Picture Styles group on the Picture Tools Format tab sports a new command, Picture Layout. Here you can you apply the look of a SmartArt picture layout to an individual picture. Each layout includes a graphic layout and a text placeholder. The result can be a lot more compelling than just inserting a picture and adding a caption. Once you apply a Picture Layout, you can access all the SmartArt editing and formatting tools on the SmartArt Tools tabs. The only difference is that your graphic contains just a single picture. Here's a picture with the Circle Picture Hierarchy layout applied. It uses the cropped circular layout and includes a place for text, but it's just one graphic, without the connecting lines and additional picture and text placeholders of the full SmartArt graphic.

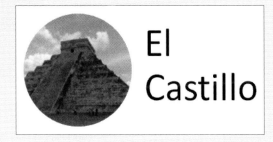

El Castillo

Tap into more powerful graphics

When you work with pictures in Word 2010, you might think you're using an image editor instead of a Word processor. In addition to all the formatting and enhancements you can make, you can now make more intensive changes to a picture file. The cropping feature has been pumped up to offer more options and greater control, and a new Remove Background feature is available. Word now offers tools for capturing screenshots and inserting them instantly in the current document. You can choose between capturing an image of any open window on your computer or doing a custom clipping.

Apply It in SAM!

- Remove the background of a picture
- Insert a screen capture of the current window
- Take a custom screen clipping

Remove the background of a picture

1. **With a picture selected, click the Picture Tools Format tab on the Ribbon. In the Adjust group, click the Remove Background button. A marquee indicates the area that will remain in the picture. The shading indicates the area that will be removed.**

2. **Make your adjustments to the picture. Use tools on the Background Remove tab to refine your selections. Your drawing doesn't have to be absolutely precise; Word makes selections based on the areas you click and drag across.**

Click this button, then click or drag an area marked for deletion if you want to keep it

If you change your mind about a mark, click this button, then click the mark you want to remove

Drag any marquee handle to resize the marquee so it best fits the area you want to keep

Click this button, then click an area that you want to crop

All shaded areas will be removed

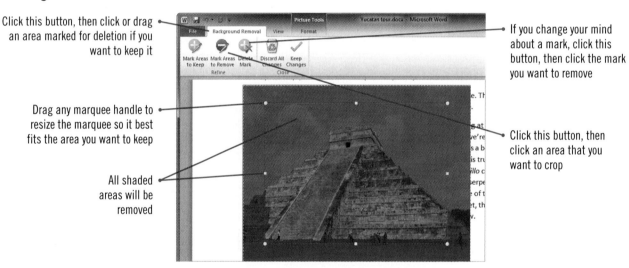

3. **Click the Keep Changes button in the Close group to apply your changes; or, click the Discard All Changes button to cancel the changes and restore the picture completely.**

4. **Click away from the picture to deselect it.**

Text wraps around pyramid

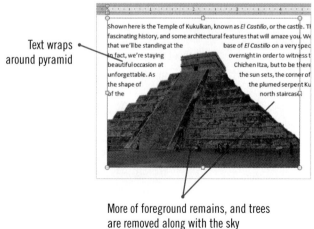

More of foreground remains, and trees are removed along with the sky

QUICK TIP

Compressing a picture affects the amount of detail in a picture, so if you plan to compress pictures in your document, do so *before* removing the background of a picture.

Apply custom cropping

1. With a picture selected, click the Picture Tools Format tab, click the Crop arrow in the Size group, click Crop to Shape, then click a shape.

2. Make any additional customizations to the crop.

Word 2010

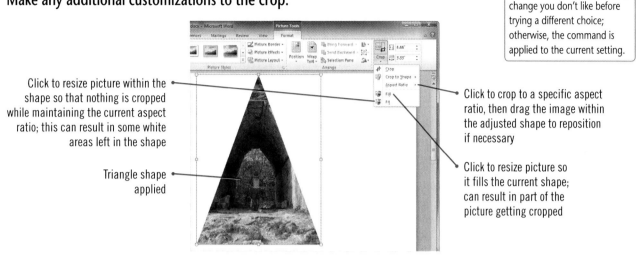

Click to resize picture within the shape so that nothing is cropped while maintaining the current aspect ratio; this can result in some white areas left in the shape

Triangle shape applied

Click to crop to a specific aspect ratio, then drag the image within the adjusted shape to reposition if necessary

Click to resize picture so it fills the current shape; can result in part of the picture getting cropped

3. When you're finished, click away from the picture to deselect it.

Insert a screenshot or clipping

1. Click in the document where you want to insert the screenshot or clipping.

2. Click the Insert tab on the Ribbon, then click Screenshot in the Illustrations group. A gallery opens, displaying all the windows currently open on your computer.

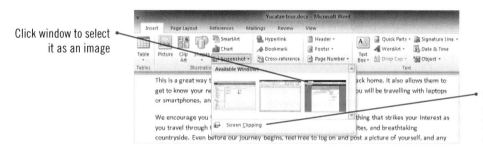

Click window to select it as an image

Click to insert a custom clipping instead of an entire window

3. Click any window in the gallery, or click Screen Clipping below the image gallery, then use the crosshair pointer + to create a marquee around the area you want to capture. When you release the mouse button, the image is inserted at the location of the insertion point and the Picture Tools Format tab opens.

Click any tool to make formatting changes to inserted image

Inserted image

Translate text and documents

The translation tools in Word enhance your global communicate skills. In addition to using the Research pane to translate selected words or phrases, you can use the new Translate Document feature to translate entire documents instantly, using machine translation services available over the Internet. For times when you want to translate a word or phrase at a time into another language, you can turn on the Mini Translator; this is a huge help when you're writing in another language and just need occasional help as you go.

Translate a document

1. With the document open, click the Review tab on the Ribbon.

2. Click the Translate button 📖 in the Language group. In the Translate menu, the Translate Document command displays any current settings for translation. In this example, Word is set to translate from English (U.S.) to Japanese. If you have not previously set language options, this area is blank.

QUICK TIP
The Translate Selected text command works like the Translate command in Word 2007; clicking it opens the Research pane with the Translation option selected.

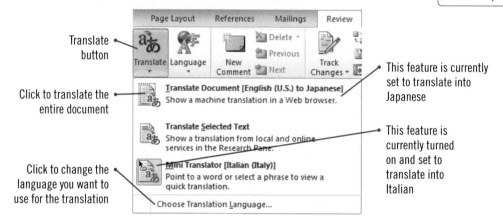

Translate button

Click to translate the entire document

Click to change the language you want to use for the translation

This feature is currently set to translate into Japanese

This feature is currently turned on and set to translate into Italian

3. Click Translate Document. A dialog box opens to inform you that your text will be sent over the Internet in an unencrypted form to a translation service.

QUICK TIP
The Translate Document and Mini Translation features send your text to a machine translation service on the Web; because the text is unencrypted, it could potentially be viewed by others on the Internet.

Collaborating with Word 2007 users

When you create a new document in Word 2010, you'll see the .docx file extension that was introduced in Word 2007. However, there's a difference between .docx documents created in Word 2007 and those created in Word 2010. A .docx document created in Word 2010 may contain elements created by features new in Word 2010, so it might not display properly in earlier versions of Word. So, before you send a document to a Word 2007 user, use the Compatibility Checker on the Info Page to check for issues; make sure that Word 2007 is selected in the Select versions to show list.

If you open a document in Word 2010 that was created in Word 2007, the document opens in Compatibility mode and any new 2010 features are unavailable. That's just in case this document will be going back to a 2007 user. You can continue working on the document in Compatibility mode, and new features (such as the Background Removal tool) will be unavailable. If you're confident that you won't need to send this document back to someone working in an older version, you can convert it to Word 2010. To do that, click the File tab on the Ribbon. On the Info page, click the Convert button.

4. If you are comfortable sending the text over the Internet, click Send. The document is translated.

Japanese translation of current document

5. If you wish, select the translated text, copy it, then paste it in your document.

Translate a word or phrase

1. With the document open, click the Review tab on the Ribbon, then in the Language group, click the Translate button 🗚. In the Translate menu, the Mini Translator command displays the current language it's set to translate to. If you have not previously chosen a language, this area is blank.

2. Click Mini Translator. This command is a toggle; clicking it once turns it on, and clicking it when it is on turns it off.

3. Point to a word or phrase. A translation ScreenTip opens. If you select more than one word and then point to the selection, the ScreenTip translates the entire phrase if possible. If a translation is not available, the ScreenTip reads, "No results were found."

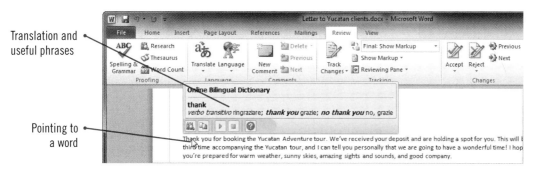

Translation and useful phrases

Pointing to a word

4. To stop seeing Translation ScreenTips, click the Translate button, then click the Mini Translator to deactivate it.

Setting translation languages

Before using the Translate Document feature or Mini Translator, you may want to set language options. To do so, click the Review tab on the Ribbon, click the Translate button in the Translate menu, then click Choose Translation Language. The Translation Language Options dialog box opens. In the list on the left, click the feature you want to set translation languages for. The Translate Document feature allows you to set a both a language to translate from and a language to translate into. The Mini Translator allows you to set only a language to translate into. Next, if setting languages for the Translate Document features, click the From list arrow, choose a language, click the To list arrow, choose a language, then click OK. For the Mini Translator, click the Translate to list arrow, then click a language. Click OK, then click the Translate button again to open the menu and continue using the translation features.

Explore more Word improvements

In addition to what you've already explored, there are more new features and improvements in Word. Many of these integrate existing tools with brand new ones into a user interface that better supports your workflow. For example, the Info page brings together features from the Save As dialog box, the Prepare command on the Office menu, and the Protect Document command from the Review tab, as well as other features, because these are all related to information you might want to view or change about the way you and others interact with your document.

Get Help

1. Click the File tab on the Ribbon, then click Help on the Navigation bar. The Help page is a the one-stop shop for getting support and performing other Office-related tasks. See the table for details.

2. To get help on a particular feature or task, click Microsoft Office Help in the middle pane. The support page for Word opens. If a document is open, Word displays additional links geared to what you might need help with.

QUICK TIP
You can open the Word Help window any time by clicking the Help icon ? on the Ribbon.

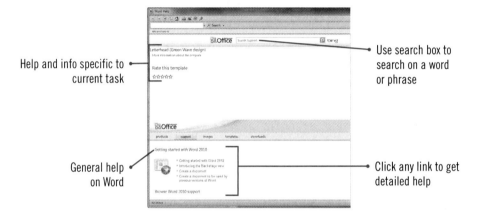

Help and info specific to current task

Use search box to search on a word or phrase

General help on Word

Click any link to get detailed help

3. Click any link to get more information.

Options available on the Help page in Backstage view

option	use to
Microsoft Office Help	Get online help on all Word features through tutorials and instructions, Microsoft Office training, and other resources; browse images, templates, and products available for download
Getting Started	Learn basic Word 2010 tasks and get specific guidance on what's changed from previous versions
Contact Us	Open the Microsoft Support site, where you can get help with customer-related issues
Options	Review and change program options, including your user name, document display settings, and more
Check for Updates	Make sure you're running the most recent version of Office
Product activation status	Find out what flavor of Office is installed, and review or change your product key
About Microsoft Word	Find out what version of Word is currently running, see your product ID, and link to customer service

Get information on a document

1. Click the File tab on the Ribbon to open Backstage view. The Info tab appears with properties for the current document on the right.

Info tab

Click to run a report on potential privacy, accessibility, or compatibility issues

Click to change how properties are displayed

Click a field to edit it

Some informational fields cannot be edited

2. To run a detailed report, click the Check for Issues button, then click an option. As you run each report, read the report and follow the instructions to resolve any issues. For example, here we're checking the accessibility of the current document. The Accessibility Checker lets you click through each issue and learn how to fix it.

Potential problem selected in document

Potential problem

Explains potential problem

Explains how to fix potential problem

Publish the current document as a blog post

1. Click the File tab on the Ribbon to open Backstage view, then click Save & Send on the Navigation bar.

2. Click Publish as Blog Post in the center pane, then click the Publish as Blog post button. A copy of the current document opens, and the Blog Post tab opens on the Ribbon. Click Publish in the Blog group to complete the post.

> **QUICK TIP**
> If you have more than one blog account, use the Manage Accounts button to specify which blog to publish this post to.

Click to view the home page of your blog

Click to enter a title for your blog post

Make any additional changes to your post

Click to view or edit a blog post already published to your blog

Word 2010

Word 2010 Quick Reference

To Do This	Go Here	To Do This	Go Here
Add alt text to a picture	Picture Tools Format tab	dialog box launcher	Navigate and rearrange headings	Navigation pane
Apply a picture layout	Picture Tools Format tab	Picture Styles group	Open a document	File tab	Open command File tab	Recent
Apply artistic effects	Picture Tools Format tab	Adjust group	Open a draft version of a document (.asd format)	File tab	Info	Manage Versions	Recover Draft Versions
Change a picture	Picture Tools Format tab	Adjust group	Open an autosaved version of a document	File tab	Info	Versions
Change picture brightness or contrast	Picture Tools Format tab	Adjust group	Corrections	Preview and print	File tab	Print
Change picture shape	Picture Tools Format tab	Size group	Crop menu	Crop to Shape	Protect a document	File tab	Info	Protect Document
Change translation language	Review tab	Language group	Translate button	Publish a document as a blog post	File tab	Save & Send
Check accessibility or compatibility	File tab	Info tab	Check for Issues button	Recolor a picture	Picture Tools Format tab	Adjust group	Color
Compress a picture	Picture Tools Format tab	Adjust group	Compress Pictures	Remove the background of a picture	Picture Tools Format tab	Adjust group
Create a document	File tab	New	Reset a picture	Picture Tools Format tab	Adjust group
Crop a picture	Picture Tools Format tab	Size group	Crop menu	Save a document	File tab	Save As
E-mail a document	File tab	Save & Send tab	Send Using E-mail	Save a document to a shared location	File tab	Save & Send
Get Help	File tab	Help Help icon on Ribbon	Search for text, graphics and other elements	Home tab	Editing group	Find
Insert a screenshot or custom clipping	Insert tab	Illustrations group	Screenshot	Sharpen or soften a picture	Picture Tools Format tab	Adjust group	Corrections menu
Insert SmartArt	Insert tab	Illustrations group	SmartArt	Translate text	Review tab	Language group	Translate menu
Navigate a document	View tab	Navigation Pane check box	View document properties	File tab	Info

2 Upgrading to Excel 2010

When you upgrade to Microsoft Excel 2010, you'll find it continues to offer the tab interface you're familiar with from Excel 2007. To improve usability, several of the command locations have changed. After you get acquainted with the new organization, you should be just as productive as you were in Excel 2007. ■ ■ ▪ As you review these lessons, you will be able to practice many of the skills using Skills Assessment Manager (SAM). The lessons will cover SAM skills and tasks as outlined in this table:

Lesson	SAM Tasks
Picture your data with sparklines	■ Create a sparkline for a range of numeric cells ■ Apply a sparkline style ■ Modify the format of a sparkline
Learn new conditional formatting options	■ Apply conditional formatting to a range of cells ■ Edit a conditional formatting rule
Filter PivotTables using slicers	■ In a PivotTable, insert a slicer for one category ■ Use the slicer to display the PivotTable data for a category ■ Cancel a filter ■ Delete the slicer
Make workbooks accessible	■ Check a workbook's accessibility ■ Add alternate text to a chart
Manage workbooks using Backstage view	■ Locate and open an existing workbook ■ Save a file to a different location ■ Save a workbook with a new name ■ Print a worksheet ■ Close a workbook and exit Excel
Work with the Excel Web App	■ Save a workbook to SkyDrive ■ Edit data in an online workbook
Use other Excel improvements	■ Customize the Ribbon
Other Lessons	
Share workbooks using Backstage view	

Picture your data with sparklines

As you know, Excel charts are a great way to get a picture of your data to see trends and other patterns. But sometimes you want to summarize a trend in a small amount of space. **Sparklines** are tiny charts that fit inside one cell. They give you a quick snapshot of the "story" your data has to tell. You can place them near, or even behind, the data itself, so they act as a handy and compact reference. You can also use them to highlight maximum or minimum values. After you create a sparkline, you can choose a style for it and then customize the way it looks. Like any Excel chart, sparklines respond to changes you make to the underlying data.

Insert a sparkline

1. Select the range that contains the data you want to graph as one or more sparklines.

2. Click the Insert tab, then in the Sparklines group, click the sparkline type you want. See the table for a list of sparkline types. The Create Sparklines dialog box opens, with the data range you selected in the Data Range text box.

3. Select the cell or range where you want to insert the sparkline. The cell address appears in the Location Range text box.

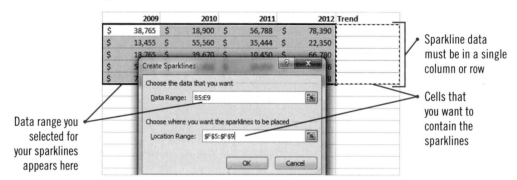

Data range you selected for your sparklines appears here

Sparkline data must be in a single column or row

Cells that you want to contain the sparklines

4. Click OK. Sparklines appear in the Location Range cells you selected.

	2009		2010		2011		2012	Trend
$	38,765	$	18,900	$	56,788	$	78,390	
$	13,455	$	55,560	$	35,444	$	22,350	
$	18,765	$	39,670	$	10,450	$	66,780	
$	55,670	$	15,432	$	19,654	$	44,236	
$	75,930	$	26,444	$	39,876	$	45,678	

Sparklines reflect data trends

Apply a sparkline style

1. Click a cell in the range that contains your sparklines.

2. Click the Sparkline Tools Design tab if necessary.

3. Click a sparkline style in the Style group.

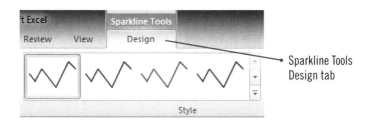

Sparkline Tools
Design tab

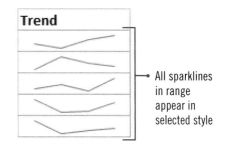

All sparklines
in range
appear in
selected style

Change the look of a sparkline

1. Click a cell in the range that contains the sparklines.

2. Choose an option from one of the groups on the Sparkline Tools Design tab.

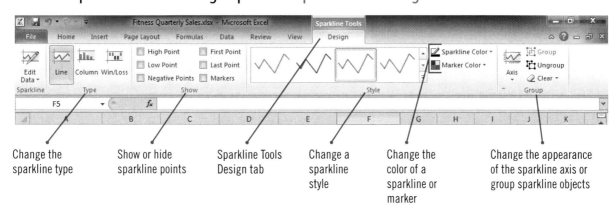

Change the sparkline type

Show or hide sparkline points

Sparkline Tools Design tab

Change a sparkline style

Change the color of a sparkline or marker

Change the appearance of the sparkline axis or group sparkline objects

Here is an example of a customized sparkline:

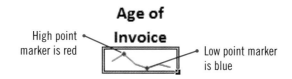

High point marker is red

Age of Invoice

Low point marker is blue

Types of Sparklines

sparkline type	looks like
Line	
Column	
Win/Loss	

Customizing sparklines for your data

If any of your data range cells are empty, you can tell Excel how you want sparklines to appear, if at all, for those cells. On the Sparkline Tools Design tab, click the Edit Data list arrow in the Sparkline group, then click Hidden & Empty Cells. In the dialog box, click an option button to indicate whether you want empty cells to be shown as gaps, zero, or with connecting lines between the data points.

Learn new conditional formatting options

Conditional formatting in Excel 2007 formatted your cells automatically, depending on the values in the cells. You could use colors, data bars, and icons to give your audience an easy way to see the meaning and overall trends in your data. Excel 2010 gives you richer options: You can now use stars, triangles, and boxes as conditional formatting icons. Plus, you can combine different types of icons within one data range or have no conditional formatting in selected cells. See the table below for new color scale choices.

Apply a new conditional format

1. Select the range containing the data you want to format, then click the Home tab.
2. Click the Conditional Formatting button in the Styles group, then point to Icon Sets.
3. Choose a new icon format: 3 Triangles ▲ ━ ▼ , 3 Stars ☆ ☆ ☆ , or 5 boxes ▦ ▦ ▦ ▦ ▦ .

	Sales
January	▲ 22,543.00
February	━ 11,799.00
March	━ 6,546.00
April	▼ (6,754.00)
May	▼ 2,456.00
June	━ 10,234.00

Range formatted with new 3 Triangles icon set

Combine conditional formats in a custom rule

1. Select the range containing the data you want to format.
2. Click the Conditional Formatting button in the Styles group, then click New Rule to open the New Formatting Rule dialog box.
3. Click the Format Style list arrow, click Icon Sets, click the Icon Style list arrow, and then choose an icon style.
4. For each icon you want to customize, click that icon's list arrow, click another icon, then click OK.

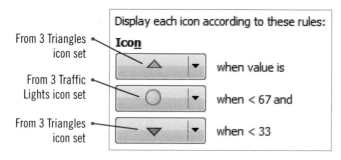

From 3 Triangles icon set

From 3 Traffic Lights icon set

From 3 Triangles icon set

Display each icon according to these rules:

Icon

△ — when value is

○ — when < 67 and

▽ — when < 33

The following data range is formatted with this custom rule:

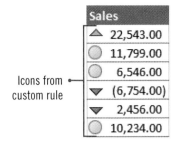

Icons from custom rule

Display conditional formatting in selected cells

1. Select the range containing the data you want to format, then click the Home tab.
2. Click the Conditional Formatting button in the Styles group, then click the New Rule button to open the New Formatting Rule dialog box.
3. Click the Format Style list arrow, click Icon Sets, click the Icon Style list arrow, and then choose an icon style.
4. Under Icon, click the list arrow next to the icon you want to hide, then click No Cell Icon.

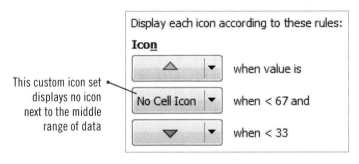

This custom icon set displays no icon next to the middle range of data

Only values in the top third and bottom third of the data range display icons

New Color Scale Formatting Options

color scale icon	color scale name	color scale icon	color scale name
	Green – White – Red		White – Red
	Red – White – Green		Red – White
	Blue – White – Red		Green – White
	Red – White – Blue		White – Green

Learning new data bar options

Data bars in Excel 2007 had gradient fills; you can now choose solid fills in any color you prefer. You can also add data bar borders in any color. In addition, data bars can extend to the left or the right of a vertical line in the cell. Negative values appear on the opposite side of a vertical line within the cell. In this figure, the negative amount shows clearly as a red bar on the right side of the line.

Sales
22,543.00
11,799.00
6,546.00
(6,754.00)
2,456.00

Filter PivotTables using slicers

PivotTables have always let you filter large sets of data using drop-down lists so you can display only the data you want. But it is sometimes difficult to see how the PivotTable filters the data—especially when you filter on more than one value. Now filtering is easier (and more fun) using slicers. **Slicers** are formatted button sets you create next to your PivotTables. They're perfect for inexperienced Excel users who want to analyze their data. Each slicer button represents a PivotTable field. You can click the slicer buttons to filter data quickly and easily. For example, a slicer for City values might have buttons for New York, Chicago, and Sydney. Click a city name on the slicer to see PivotTable data for that city. Add another slicer to the PivotTable if you need one to display data for a particular sales rep, for example.

Insert a slicer for one field

1. Click in the PivotTable, then click the PivotTable Tools Options tab, if necessary.
2. Click the Insert Slicer button in the Sort & Filter group. The Insert Slicers dialog box opens, listing the fields in the PivotTable.
3. Click the field name(s) you want to use to filter your data, then click OK.

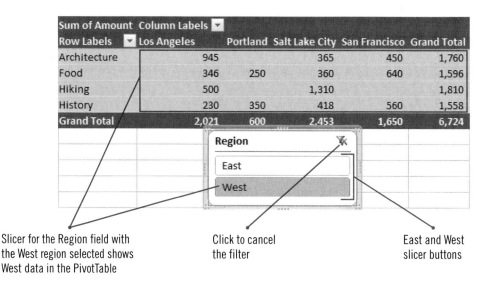

Slicer for the Region field with the West region selected shows West data in the PivotTable

Click to cancel the filter

East and West slicer buttons

Filter data using a slicer

1. Click a slicer button to change the data displayed in the PivotTable.

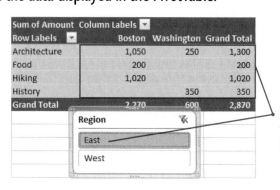

Clicking the slicer button for the East region shows East data in the PivotTable

Filter with multiple slicers

1. Click in the PivotTable, then click the PivotTable Tools Options tab, if necessary.

2. Click the Insert Slicer button in the Sort & Filter group, click a second field name, click OK, then move the slicer if necessary.

3. Click a field name in the second slicer, then click OK.

> **QUICK TIP**
> To delete a slicer, click its title bar, then press [Delete].

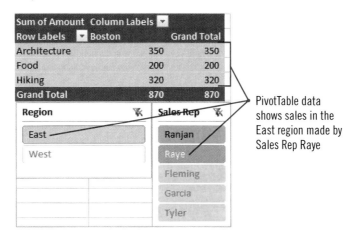

PivotTable data shows sales in the East region made by Sales Rep Raye

Format a slicer

1. Click the edge of a slicer to select it and display the Slicer Tools Options tab.

2. Click the Slicer Tools Options tab, then click a style in the Slicer Styles group to apply that style to the slicer.

> **QUICK TIP**
> To hide a slicer, select it, click the Selection Pane button in the Arrange group, then click the Visibility icon 👁 next to the slicer you want to hide.

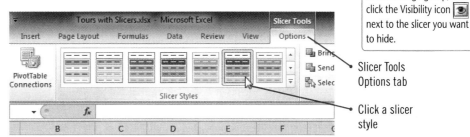

Slicer Tools Options tab

Click a slicer style

Customizing slicers

Slicers are worksheet objects that you can move, overlap, and format. To format a slicer, select it and use the settings on the Slicer Tools Options tab. Use the Columns setting in the Buttons group to create a slicer with buttons arranged horizontally. Change a slicer's caption in the Slicer Caption setting in the Slicer group. To create your own slicer style, click the Slicer Styles More button in the Slicer Styles group, then click New Slicer Style. Click an element in the Slicer Element list, then click the Format button and assign a font, color, border, or fill. You can set the appearance of items according to their state: when they are selected or unselected, when the mouse pointer hovers over them, and when they have data or do not.

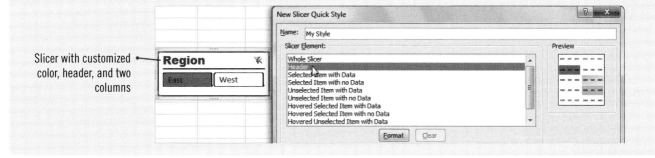

Slicer with customized color, header, and two columns

Make workbooks accessible

When you share a workbook with others, remember that not everyone has full mobility or vision. Now you can use Excel tools to make your shared workbooks usable by more people. The **Accessibility Checker** scans your workbook and tells you if any workbook content might be difficult for people with disabilities. For example, you should always assign names to your worksheets and worksheet objects so machines that read documents can describe the objects to the user. The Accessibility Checker lists objects that don't have names. You name worksheet objects by giving them **alternate text**, descriptive text that machines can read. For example, you might assign the name *2013 Sales Chart* to a chart to describe its contents. You can add alternate text to any worksheet object, including charts, shapes, SmartArt, tables, and PivotTables.

Check a workbook's accessibility

1. Click the File tab, then in the center pane, click the Check for Issues button.

2. Click Check Accessibility. The Accessibility Checker scans the workbook to find content that people with disabilities might find difficult to read.

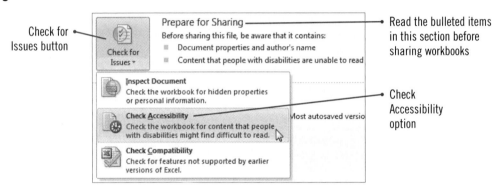

Check for Issues button

Read the bulleted items in this section before sharing workbooks

Check Accessibility option

3. Read the Accessibility Checker pane on the right side of the Excel window.

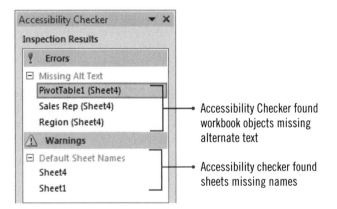

Accessibility Checker found workbook objects missing alternate text

Accessibility checker found sheets missing names

Make worksheet objects accessible

1. Right-click a PivotTable, then click PivotTable Options.
2. In the PivotTable Options dialog box, click the Alt Text tab.
3. Type a title and description for the PivotTable, then click OK.

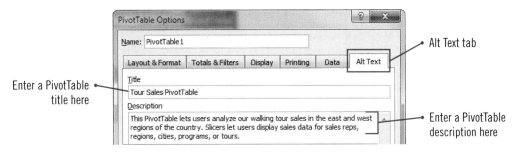

Alt Text tab

Enter a PivotTable title here

Enter a PivotTable description here

Select an accessibility issue and find a solution

1. Click an accessibility issue in the Accessibility Checker pane.

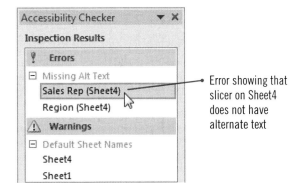

Error showing that slicer on Sheet4 does not have alternate text

2. In the Additional Information section of the Accessibility Checker pane, read the explanation of why and how you should fix the issue.

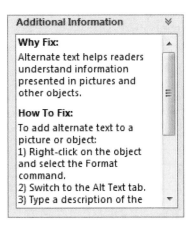

QUICK TIP

To add alternative text to a chart, picture, or other object, right-click the object, click a Format command, then click the Alt Text option. For a table or PivotTable, click Alternative Text or Alt Text.

Preparing for sharing workbooks

Accessibility checking is one way Excel 2010 helps you prepare your workbooks for sharing. Excel also lets you inspect your document for hidden properties and personal information and for compatibility with earlier versions of Excel. If you inspect your workbooks for all three of these issues, you ensure that your workbooks are in good shape to share with others on a company intranet or on the Web.

Manage workbooks using Backstage view

To open, save, print, and close your Excel workbooks, Excel 2010 provides a new feature called Backstage view. **Backstage view** is a work area you can display by clicking the new **File tab** on the Ribbon. The File tab replaces the Office button in Excel 2007. You'll find many everyday file management tasks here, plus some others, such as getting help and preparing workbooks for sharing with others. You click commands on the **Navigation bar** to handle document tasks.

Open, save, and close workbooks

1. Click the File tab on the Ribbon. Backstage view opens, displaying the Navigation bar on the left.

File tab •

2. View the commands at the top of the Navigation bar. You use these commands to save, open, and close workbooks, as shown in the figure below.

3. Click Recent on the Navigation bar to see a list of recently used documents, then click the name of the workbook you want to open.

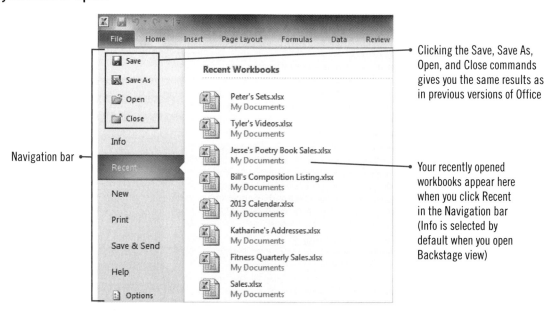

4. Click Save As in the Navigation bar to open the Save As dialog box; to save a file to a different location, navigate to the location using the Address bar or the list of locations. To save a file with a new name, type the name in the File name text box, then click Save.

Create a new, blank document

1. Click the File tab if necessary, then click New on the Navigation bar.
2. Click Blank workbook in the center pane.

3. Click Create in the right pane to open a new, blank workbook.

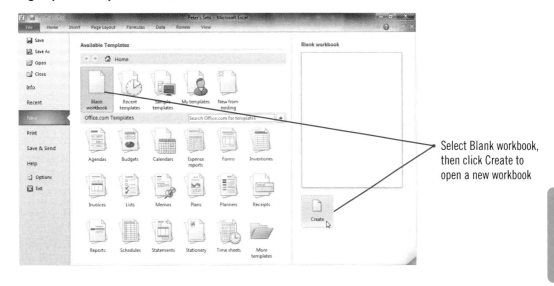

Select Blank workbook, then click Create to open a new workbook

Preview and print a document, then exit Excel

1. Open a workbook, click the File tab, then click Print on the Navigation bar.

Click the Print button to print with the current settings

Print options replace the Print dialog box in earlier versions of Excel

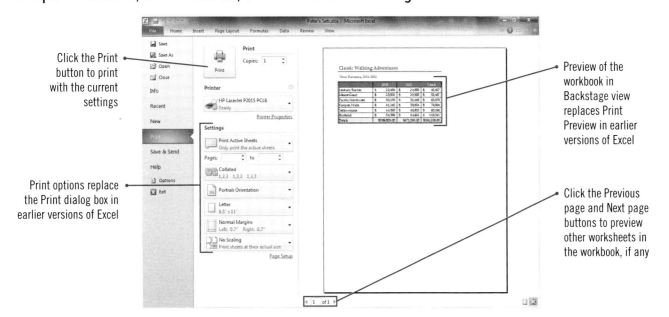

Preview of the workbook in Backstage view replaces Print Preview in earlier versions of Excel

Click the Previous page and Next page buttons to preview other worksheets in the workbook, if any

2. If necessary, select a print option in the Settings area.

Print Active Sheets button

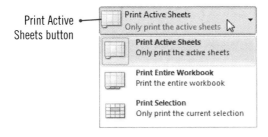

3. When you are finished making print selections, click the Print button in the center pane to print your document.

4. Click the File tab, then click Exit to close the Excel program.

Work with the Excel Web App

If you are using a computer that doesn't have Excel installed on it, you can still edit workbooks using many Excel tools available in the Excel Web App. The **Excel Web App** is the free, lighter version of Excel on the Web, available to the public. With the Excel Web App, you can edit online Excel files using a Web browser on your computer or your mobile phone. First, you save or upload an Excel file to your Windows Live SkyDrive or a SharePoint server. The **Windows Live SkyDrive** is a sharing and file-storage Web site that anyone can access for free, and is located at http://skydrive.live.com. Next, go to your SkyDrive and open the posted file, which automatically starts the Excel Web App. Because the program is on the Web, you don't have to download any software. You can use the Web App to enter and edit the file's data and work with its formulas. You can sort and filter data in tables or PivotTables. Because the Excel Web App contains a subset of the full Excel program features, some Excel features are not supported.

Save a workbook to Windows Live SkyDrive

1. Click the File tab, then click Save & Send on the Navigation bar.
2. Click Save to Web in the center pane, then click the Sign In button in the right pane.

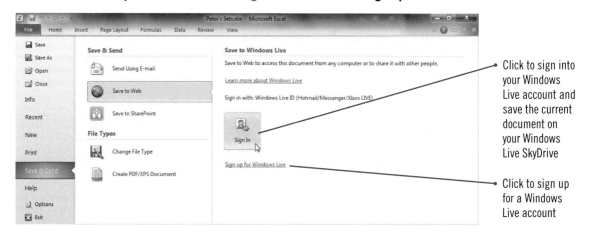

Click to sign into your Windows Live account and save the current document on your Windows Live SkyDrive

Click to sign up for a Windows Live account

3. Enter your Windows Live ID user name and password, click OK, then click the Windows Live link.
4. Click the folder on your SkyDrive where you want to save the document, then click the Save As button.

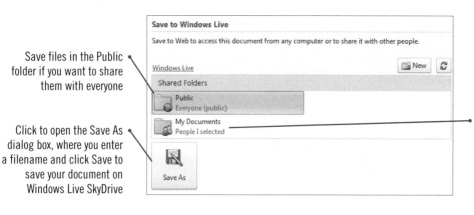

Save files in the Public folder if you want to share them with everyone

Click to open the Save As dialog box, where you enter a filename and click Save to save your document on Windows Live SkyDrive

Save files in the My Documents folder if you want to share them with only people you specify

Edit data using the Excel Web App

1. Save your file to your Windows Live SkyDrive, then close the workbook and Excel.

2. Using a Web browser, sign into your Windows Live SkyDrive account (http://skydrive.live.com), then open the folder where you saved your Excel file.

3. Point to the file until the pointer becomes the hand icon, then click once.

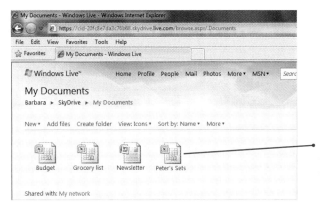

Click an Excel file on your SkyDrive to start the Excel Web App

4. Click the large Excel icon to view the workbook, click Edit in Browser to open the workbook in the Excel Web App, then enter your Windows Live ID if necessary.

Excel Web App Ribbon has File, Home, and Insert tabs

Use Ribbon commands to edit and format data

If available, use filter list arrows or slicers to interact with data

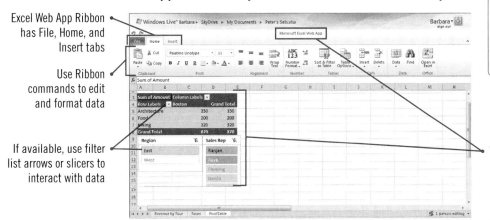

Workbook opens in Excel Web App

5. Use the buttons on the Home and Insert tabs to edit the data.

QUICK TIP
You don't need to use a Save command to save changes on your SkyDrive. All changes are saved automatically.

QUICK TIP
Instead of clicking the large Excel icon, you can click the View or Edit button above the icon. If necessary, click Accept to accept the Microsoft Service Agreement.

QUICK TIP
The Excel Web App does not display SmartArt graphics or pictures in workbooks.

Using Selected Excel Web App File Tab Commands

file tab command	description
Open in Excel	Open the current Excel Web App file in the full Excel program (if available on your computer)
Save As	Save the workbook to any location with a new name on Windows Live SkyDrive
Download a Snapshot	Save a picture of the workbook with values and formatting, but not formulas
Download a Copy	Save a copy of the workbook to your computer

Keeping in touch with Excel Mobile 2010

You can open your workbooks from any smartphone that uses Windows Mobile 6.5. Office Mobile 2010 lets you work with your files any way, even with a touch-screen device. Excel Mobile 2010 lets you edit workbooks, whether they are in an e-mail message or stored on your phone. You can also use your smartphone browser to view Excel workbooks you have published to a SharePoint server or Windows Live services.

Excel 2010

Use other Excel improvements

Excel 2010 has other improvements that help to increase your productivity. Some of these features are shared with Word, PowerPoint, and Access, and others are specific to Excel. Other chapters in this book describe the Picture tools, Screenshot tool, and the new SmartArt features in Word and PowerPoint. You can also use these tools in Excel when you want to create a visual effect. The Screenshot tools let you insert a graphic of an open window or capture and paste a screen shot of another document.

Apply It in SAM

■ Customize the Ribbon

Use picture tools

1. Click a photo on your worksheet.
2. On the Picture Tools Format tab, click Artistic Effects in the Adjust group, then choose an effect.

Preview of Artistic effects to apply to the selected photo

Cutout artistic effect applied

Create screen shots

1. Click the Insert tab, then click the Screenshot button in the Illustrations group.
2. Click Screen Clipping, then drag to capture a screen portion.

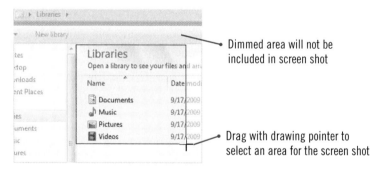

Dimmed area will not be included in screen shot

Drag with drawing pointer to select an area for the screen shot

Use SmartArt layouts

1. Click the Insert tab, then click the SmartArt button in the Illustrations group.
2. Click Picture in the list of layout types, select a picture layout, then click OK.

3. Click each picture placeholder and choose a picture.

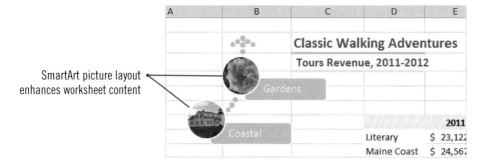

SmartArt picture layout enhances worksheet content

Use Paste Preview

1. Select a cell or range that contains data.
2. Click the Copy button in the Clipboard group.
3. Click the Paste list arrow, point to a paste option, then click the option you want.

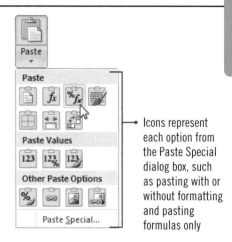

Icons represent each option from the Paste Special dialog box, such as pasting with or without formatting and pasting formulas only

Customize the Ribbon

1. Click the File tab, then click Options.
2. Click Customize Ribbon. You can only add commands to a new custom group or a new tab.
3. In the right pane, click the tab or group you want to modify, then click New Tab or New Group.
4. Click a command in the left pane, then click Add to add the command button to the selected tab or group.

Click Add to add the command to the selected location

Fill Color command button added to new group on a new tab

Using the improved Solver

The Solver add-in is a companion to the Excel program that helps you calculate complex what-if analyses called models. For example, you might want to calculate an optimum project budget while keeping varying expenses, such as advertising and equipment, at certain maximum levels. Excel 2010 features a new version of the Solver add-in that is easier to use and contains more comprehensive reports as well as faster, more efficient methods of calculating results. You can learn more by visiting www.solver.com.

Share workbooks using Backstage view

You can use Backstage view as a launching point to share your Excel workbooks with others. You can e-mail workbooks or publish them online so others can use them. When you save a workbook to a Windows Live SkyDrive, you can convert it to another format. Using the Excel Web App, you can also collaborate with others by editing a workbook at the same time as another user. For more information on Windows Live SkyDrive, see the appendix "Working with Windows Live and Office Web Apps."

Send a workbook using e-mail

1. Click the File tab, then click Save & Send on the Navigation bar.

Send Using E-mail option selected, which displays e-mail options in the right pane

Click a button to convert your Excel document to one of these formats and open an e-mail with the converted document attached

2. Click Send Using E-mail in the center pane, then click a button in the right pane.

Create a PDF file

1. On the File tab, click Save & Send on the Navigation bar.
2. Click Create PDF/XPS Document in the center pane.
3. Click the Create PDF/XPS button in the right pane.
4. Choose a location and filename, then click Publish.

QUICK TIP
To restrict access to your workbooks, click Info in Backstage view, then click Protect Workbook. Here you can mark the workbook as final or protect the workbook structure or contents.

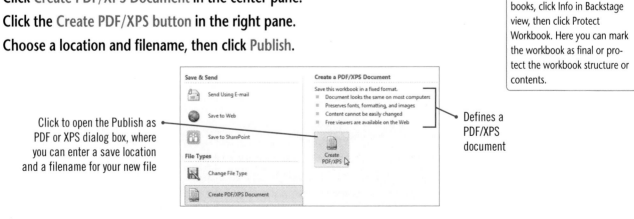

Click to open the Publish as PDF or XPS dialog box, where you can enter a save location and a filename for your new file

Defines a PDF/XPS document

Collaborate with others

1. Save a workbook to your Windows Live SkyDrive in a folder where others have permission to add, edit, and delete files.

2. Using a Web browser, open the workbook from your SkyDrive by clicking the workbook then clicking Edit.

3. Click in the Address bar to select the URL, then press [Ctrl]+[C] to copy the URL.

Open file in Excel Web App →
Click URL to select it

4. Open your e-mail program, then address an e-mail to the person you want to contribute to the workbook. This person must be part of your Windows Live network. (See the next section for instructions on adding someone to your network.)

5. Paste the URL you copied into the e-mail message, add instructions for the recipient to click the link, then send the message.

6. Return to the open workbook on your SkyDrive, then watch the right side of the status bar in the Excel Web App window. The status bar displays how many users are editing your workbook in the Web App.

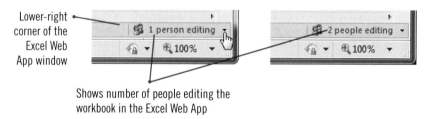

Lower-right corner of the Excel Web App window

Shows number of people editing the workbook in the Excel Web App

7. Click the list arrow to display the e-mail addresses of the people currently editing the workbook in the Excel Web App.

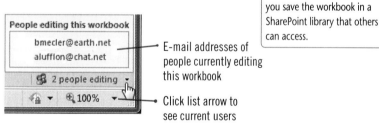

E-mail addresses of people currently editing this workbook

Click list arrow to see current users

QUICK TIP

You can also collaborate when you save the workbook in a SharePoint library that others can access.

Add someone to your Windows Live network

1. In Windows Live, click People on the Navigation bar.

2. Click Add people in the Your Network section on the left, then enter the e-mail address of someone you want to invite to your network.

3. Click the Next button, then click Send invitation. When your recipient accepts the invitation, he or she becomes part of your Windows Live network.

Managing versions using Backstage view

Like Excel 2007, Excel 2010 automatically saves versions of your workbook if you have the AutoRecover or AutoSave feature turned on. If your Excel session ends unexpectedly, Excel lets you recover the last autosaved version. Excel 2010 lets you access your earlier versions at any time, in case you forget to save or if you lose the most current version. Click the File tab, click Info on the Navigation bar, then click Manage Versions. Click Recover Unsaved Workbooks to open a dialog box letting you select the version you want.

Excel 2010 Quick Reference

To Do This	Go Here	To Do This	Go Here
Add slicer to PivotTable	PivotTable Tools Options tab | Sort & Filter group | Insert Slicer button	**Format a slicer**	Click slicer | Slicer Tools Options tab | Slicer Styles group
Cancel a slicer filter	Clear Filter button on slicer title bar	**Format a sparkline**	Click sparkline | Sparkline Tools Design tab
Change sparkline style or type	Click sparkline | Sparkline Tools Design tab	**Format data bars**	Home tab | Styles group | Conditional Formatting button | Manage Rules | Click rule | Edit Rule button | Format Style list arrow | Data Bar
Check workbook accessibility	File tab | Info | Check for Issues button | Check Accessibility	**Insert sparklines**	Insert tab | Sparklines group | Line, Column, Win/Loss buttons
Close a workbook	File tab | Close	**Manage workbook versions**	File tab | Info | Manage Versions
Collaborate on a workbook	File tab | Save & Send | Save to Web | Sign into Windows Live account | Go to SkyDrive | Click workbook | Edit button	**Open a recently used workbook**	File tab | Recent
Combine conditional format types	Home tab | Styles group | Conditional Formatting button | Manage Rules | Click rule | Edit Rule button	**Open a workbook**	File tab | Open
Convert workbook file type	File tab | Save & Send | Choose file type option	**Open Excel Help**	Ribbon | Microsoft Excel Help button *or* File tab | Help
Create new workbook	File tab | New | Blank workbook | Create button	**Open Excel Web App**	Click SkyDrive workbook | Edit or View
Create two-column slicer	Click slicer | Slicer Tools Options tab | Buttons group | Columns text box	**Preview a copied object before pasting**	Home tab | Clipboard group | Paste list arrow | Point to Paste option
Customize the Ribbon	File tab | Options | Customize Ribbon	**Preview/Print a file**	File tab | Print
Delete a slicer	Click slicer title bar | [Delete]	**Protect a workbook**	File tab | Info | Protect Workbook
Display Backstage view	File tab	**Remove conditional formatting icon**	Home tab | Styles group | Conditional Formatting button | Manage Rules | Click rule | Edit Rule button | Icon Sets | Icon list arrow | No cell icon
Edit data in Excel Web App	Windows Live SkyDrive | Workbook name | Excel icon | Edit in Browser	**Save a workbook**	File tab | Save or Save As
Edit workbook in Excel Web App	Save file to Windows Live SkyDrive | Sign into Windows Live account | Click workbook | Edit button	**Save a workbook to an earlier format**	File tab | Save & Send | Change File Type
E-mail a workbook	File tab | Save & Send | Send Using E-mail | Click a Send button	**Save a workbook to a SharePoint site**	File tab | Save & Send | Save to SharePoint
E-mail a workbook as a PDF document	File tab | Save & Send | Send Using E-mail | Send as PDF button	**Use new conditional formatting options**	Home tab | Styles group | Conditional Formatting button | Data Bars, Color Scales, Icon Sets
Exit Excel	File tab | Exit	**View workbook in Excel Web App**	Save file to SkyDrive | Sign into Windows Live account | Click workbook | View button

Upgrading to Access 2010

When you upgrade to Microsoft Access 2010, you'll find new features, enhancements to familiar tools, and a streamlined user interface. These improvements make Access 2010 easy to use for database novices and more powerful for database professionals. ▪▪▪ As you review these lessons, you will be able to practice many of the skills using Skills Assessment Manager (SAM). The lessons will cover SAM skills and tasks as outlined in this table:

Lesson	SAM Tasks	
Get started with Backstage view	▪ Start Access ▪ Create a new blank database ▪ Open a database	▪ Compact a database ▪ Back up a database
Learn shortcuts for creating tables	▪ Create a table from an application part ▪ Create a table in Datasheet view ▪ Change data type in Datasheet view	▪ Create a table in Design view ▪ Define number and currency fields in a table ▪ Change data type in Design view
Create expressions in queries	▪ Create a query using the Simple Query Wizard	▪ Create a query in Design view ▪ Add a calculated field to a query
Apply Office themes to forms and reports	▪ Create a form using the Form Wizard ▪ Create a new form in Design view ▪ Create a report using the Report Wizard	▪ Create a report in Design view ▪ Print a report
Add navigation to a database	▪ Copy a database object ▪ Rename a database object	▪ Delete a database object ▪ Group objects in the Navigation Pane
Perform repetitive tasks with macros	▪ Create a macro ▪ Undo current changes	

Other Lessons

Publish databases on the Web

Explore other Access improvements

Get started with Backstage view

Access 2010 consolidates many database management tasks on the new **File tab**, which replaces the Office button in Access 2007. Click the File tab to open **Backstage view**, where you can work with an entire database. For example, you can open or close a database, publish a database, or back it up. When you start Access, it opens in Backstage view by default and displays everything you need to get started, including collections of templates you can use to get a head start on storing and tracking your data. Open a database based on a template, and then customize it to suit your needs. You can also start from scratch by creating a standard blank database. Finally, you can create a **Web database**, which lets people use a Web browser to view, retrieve, and update data in an Access database.

Start Access

1. Click Start 🌐 , point to All Programs, click the Microsoft Office folder, then click Microsoft Access 2010.

Create a database from a template

1. On the Ribbon, click the File tab to open Backstage view, if necessary.
2. On the Navigation bar, click New, if necessary, then click Sample templates.
3. Click the desktop database template or Web database template you want to use for the new database.

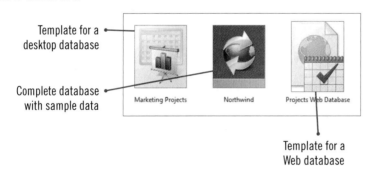

Template for a desktop database

Complete database with sample data

Marketing Projects Northwind Projects Web Database

Template for a Web database

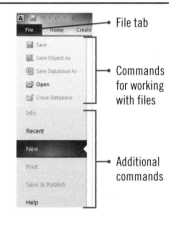

File tab

Commands for working with files

Additional commands

4. Click Create. Access creates and opens a database based on the template.

QUICK TIP
After selecting a template, you can enter a new filename for the database or use the name of the template.

Create a new blank database

1. On the Ribbon, click the File tab to open Backstage view, if necessary.
2. On the Navigation bar, click New, if necessary, then click Blank database.

QUICK TIP
If you want to download a template from Office.com, browse or search for the template in the Office.com Templates section on the New tab in Backstage view, then click Download.

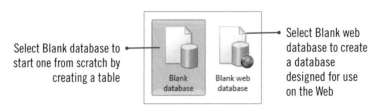

Select Blank database to start one from scratch by creating a table

Blank database

Blank web database

Select Blank web database to create a database designed for use on the Web

3. Click the Browse folder button , navigate to where you want to store your database, type the database name in the File name text box, then click OK.

4. Click the Create button.

Open a database

1. On the Ribbon, click the File tab to open Backstage view if necessary.

2. On the Navigation bar, click one of the databases you opened recently, or click Open to navigate to a different database, then double-click it.

3. To display a list of many recently opened databases, click Recent on the Navigation bar, then click a database.

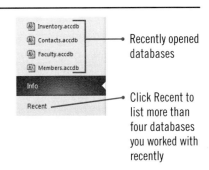

Recently opened databases

Click Recent to list more than four databases you worked with recently

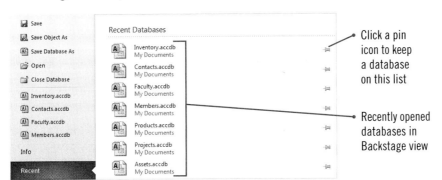

Click a pin icon to keep a database on this list

Recently opened databases in Backstage view

Compact and repair a database

1. If necessary, open the database you want to compact and repair.

2. On the Ribbon, click the File tab to open Backstage view.

3. On the Navigation bar, click Info.

4. Click the Compact & Repair Database button.

Back up a database

1. If necessary, open the database you want to back up.

2. On the Ribbon, click the File tab to open Backstage view.

3. On the Navigation bar, click Save & Publish.

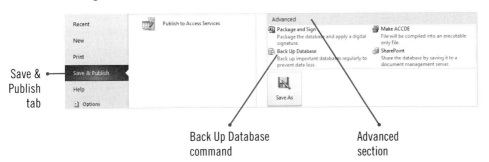

Save & Publish tab

Back Up Database command

Advanced section

4. Under Advanced, click Back Up Database, then click the Save As button. The Save As dialog box opens.

5. Review the name and location of the backup file, then click Save.

Learn shortcuts for creating tables

As in Access 2007, you can create a table in Datasheet view or in Design view. The fastest way to create a table in Datasheet view is to use an **application part**, a ready-made set of database objects. Use the new **Data Type gallery** to quickly select a data type when you create a field in Datasheet view. The Data Type gallery also includes **Quick Start fields**, which are sets of related fields. For example, the Address Quick Start field includes the Address, City, State, Zip, and Country fields.

Create a table from an application part

1. On the Ribbon, click the Create tab.
2. In the Templates group, click the Application Parts button to display a list of parts for your database.
3. In the Quick Start section, click an application part to add a table and associated forms or reports.

> **QUICK TIP**
> If necessary, you can also create a relationship with another table in your database.

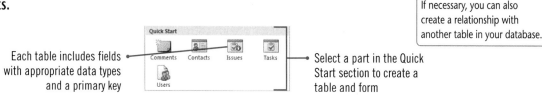

Each table includes fields with appropriate data types and a primary key

Select a part in the Quick Start section to create a table and form

Create a table in Datasheet view

1. On the Ribbon, click the Create tab.
2. In the Tables group, click the Table button. The new table opens in Datasheet view.
3. Click the first blank field below the Click to Add column heading, then enter data for this field.
4. Press [Tab] to enter data for the next field.
5. To rename fields, double-click a column heading, such as "Field1", type the field name, then press [Enter].
6. To add a new field and select the data type, click the Click to Add column heading to display a list of data types.

> **QUICK TIP**
> You can also click a field instead of a column heading, then click a data type in the Add & Delete group on the Table Tools Fields tab.

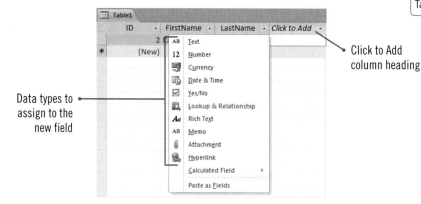

Data types to assign to the new field

Click to Add column heading

7. To apply a data type and field format at the same time, click the More Fields button in the Add & Delete group to open the Data Type gallery, then click a data type or format.

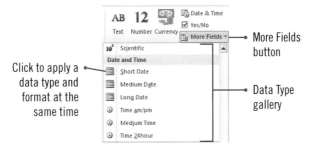

8. To add a set of related fields, scroll down in the Data Type gallery, then click a Quick Start field.

Change the data type of a field in Datasheet view

1. Click any value in the field whose data type you want to change.
2. In the Formatting group on the Table Tools Fields tab, click the Data Type arrow button.
3. Click a data type to assign it to the field.

Create a table in Design view

1. On the Ribbon, click the Create tab.
2. In the Tables group, click the Table Design button to open a new table in Design view.
3. In the first row of the Field Name column, enter a field name, press [Tab] to move to the Data Type column, then select a data type.
4. Click the Save button 💾 on the Quick Access toolbar, enter a name for the table, then click OK. If a message appears about defining a primary key, click No.

> **QUICK TIP**
> The Table Tools Design tab now includes new buttons for creating robust tables.

Define number and currency fields in a table

1. When you are creating a field in Datasheet view, click the Click to Add column heading, then click Number or Currency in the list of data types.
2. To change the data type of a field in Datasheet view, click a field value, click the Data Type list arrow in the Formatting group, then click Number or Currency.
3. To set or change the data type of a field in Design view, open the table in Design view, click in the Data Type column for the field, click the Data Type list arrow, then click Number or Currency.

> **QUICK TIP**
> Because changing the data type might cut off some or all of the data in a field, copy a table that contains data before you change a data type.

Change a data type in Design view

1. Open a table in Design view.
2. Click in the Data Type column for the field, click the Data Type list arrow, then click the new data type.

Create expressions in queries

Two of the most useful features of a database are that you can use queries to analyze your data and create expressions to perform calculations. With the new **Calculated data type**, you can create a calculated field in a table, and then add the field to other objects such as queries and forms. No matter where it appears, the field performs the calculation you need. When you create a calculated field in a table or add one to a query, you can use the redesigned **Expression Builder**. This dialog box is streamlined in Access 2010 so it's easier to use and now includes Help tools that guide you to enter expressions quickly and accurately.

Apply it in SAM!

- Create a query using the Simple Query Wizard
- Create a query in Design view
- Add a calculated field to a query

Create a query using the Simple Query Wizard

1. Click the Create tab on the Ribbon.
2. In the Queries group, click the Query Wizard button.
3. With Simple Query Wizard selected in the New Query dialog box, click OK to start the wizard.
4. Click the Tables/Queries list arrow, then click the name of a table or query.
5. To add one field to the query, click the field, then click the Select Single Field button ⟩ . To add all the fields to the query, click the Select All Fields button ⟩⟩ .
6. Click Next, enter a name for the query, then click Finish.

Create a query in Design view

1. Click the Create tab on the Ribbon.
2. In the Queries group, click the Query Design button.
3. In the Show Table dialog box, double-click the tables you want to add to the query.
4. Close the Show Table dialog box.
5. In each field list, double-click the fields you want to include in the query.

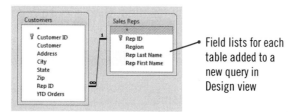

Field lists for each table added to a new query in Design view

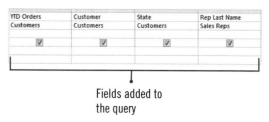

Fields added to the query

Add a calculated field to a query

1. You can create a calculated field in a table, then add the calculated field to the query using the Simple Query Wizard or Design view.

    - To add a calculated field to a table, open the table in Design view.
    - Enter a name for the field in the Field Name column.
    - In the Data Type column, select the Calculated data type. The Expression Builder dialog box opens.

> **QUICK TIP**
> Switch to Datasheet view to make sure that the calculated field works the way that you want.

- Enter the calculation you want to perform. You can select the field names from the Expression Builder list to make sure you enter them correctly.

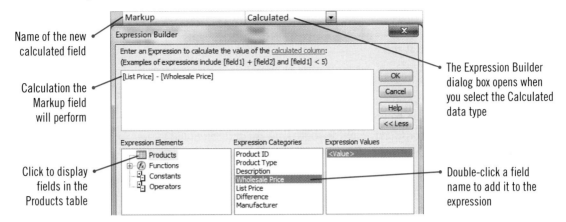

Name of the new calculated field

Calculation the Markup field will perform

Click to display fields in the Products table

The Expression Builder dialog box opens when you select the Calculated data type

Double-click a field name to add it to the expression

- Click **OK**. You can now use the calculated field in a query and other database objects.

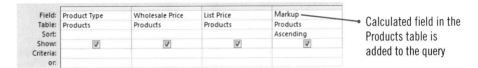

Calculated field in the Products table is added to the query

2. You can also add a calculated field to a query in Query Design view.

- With a query open in Design view, click the first available Field cell in the query design grid.

- Enter the name of the calculated field followed by a colon. For example, enter Discount: for a field that calculates a discount amount on a product.

- After the colon, enter the expression for the calculation. For example, enter [List Price] * 0.05 to calculate a discount amount that is 5 percent of the list price.

> **QUICK TIP**
> The expression in a calculated field must refer to other fields in the same table.

Getting help as you enter expressions

In Access 2010, the Expression Builder includes Help tools to guide you when entering expressions. As you begin to type an expression, Access displays a list of items such as table names and functions that you can use in the expression. This list of suggestions is called **IntelliSense**, and it helps you enter expressions quickly and accurately. While IntelliSense is displaying the names of items to include in an expression, you can click an item to display a **QuickTip**, a short description of the item. If you are entering a function, such as the IIf function, Access displays **Quick Info** to indicate the syntax of the function.

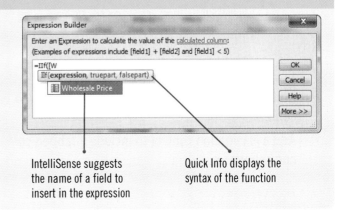

IntelliSense suggests the name of a field to insert in the expression

Quick Info displays the syntax of the function

Apply Office themes to forms and reports

The professionally designed themes introduced for Word, PowerPoint, and Excel 2007 are now included with Access 2010. When you select a **theme** in an Access 2010 database, you apply the same color scheme, fonts, and styles to your forms and reports. Using themes creates a consistent look for your database and integrates Access forms and reports with other Office 2010 documents. You can also add new types of controls to forms and reports: **Web Browser controls** and **Navigation controls**.

Apply it in SAM!

- Create a form using the Form Wizard
- Create a new form in Design view
- Create a report using the Report Wizard
- Create a report in Design View
- Print a report

Create a form using the Form Wizard

1. Click the Create tab on the Ribbon, then click the Form Wizard button in the Forms group.

Form Wizard button now appears on its own in the Forms group (not in the More Forms list)

2. Click the Tables/Queries list arrow, then click the name of a table or query to include its fields in the form. Select the fields to appear in the form, then click Next.

QUICK TIP
The Form Wizard no longer includes a step to select a style because you can now apply a theme instead.

3. Select a layout, then click Next.

4. Enter a title for the form, then click Finish.

Create a new form in Design view

1. Click the Create tab on the Ribbon, then click the Form Design button in the Forms group.

2. To add a title to the form, click the Title button in the Header/Footer group, then type the title.

3. Click the Add Existing Fields button in the Tools group to open the Field List, if necessary.

4. Drag fields from the Field List to the Details area of the form to insert text boxes and attached labels.

5. Click the More button in the Controls group to display the controls you can add to the form.

Click to add a Web Browser control

Controls to add to the form

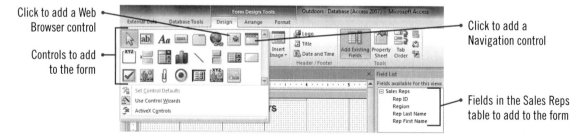

Click to add a Navigation control

Fields in the Sales Reps table to add to the form

- Add a Web Browser control to display a live Web page, such as one that shows a map or other Web content.

- Add a Navigation control to include a tabbed control with buttons you click to open other forms and reports.

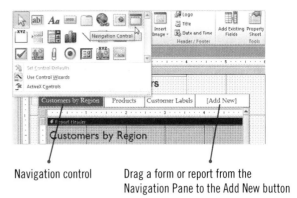

Live Web page added to a form using the Web Browser control

Navigation control

Drag a form or report from the Navigation Pane to the Add New button

Create a report using the Report Wizard

1. Click the Create tab on the Ribbon, then click the Report Wizard button in the Reports group.
2. Click the Tables/Queries list arrow, then click the name of a table or query.
3. Select the fields to add to the report, then click Next.
4. If necessary, select one or more grouping levels, click Next, select one or more sort orders, then click Next.
5. Select a layout, then click Next. Enter a title for the report, then click Finish.

QUICK TIP
The Report Wizard no longer includes a step to select an AutoFormat because you can now apply a theme instead.

Create a report in Design View

1. Click the Create tab on the Ribbon, then click the Report Design button in the Reports group.
2. To add a title to the form, click the Title button in the Header/Footer group, then type the title.
3. Click the Add Existing Fields button in the Tools group to open the Field List, if necessary.
4. Drag fields from the Field List to sections of the report.
5. Click the More button in the Controls group to display the controls you can add.
6. To apply a theme to the report, click the Themes button, point to a theme to preview its effect on the report, then click a theme.

QUICK TIP
When you select a theme, it applies to only the objects in the database created with Access 2010.

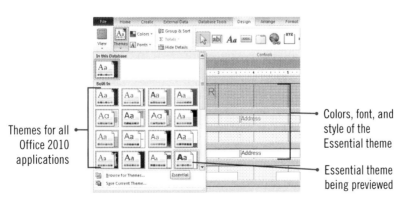

Themes for all Office 2010 applications

Colors, font, and style of the Essential theme

Essential theme being previewed

Print a report

1. On the Ribbon, click the File tab to open Backstage view.
2. On the Navigation bar, click Print.
3. Click Quick Print to print the report on the default printer, or click Print to open the Print dialog box, select settings, then click OK.

Access 2010

Add navigation to a database

Besides adding a Navigation control to a report to make it easy to open other forms and reports, you can create a **Navigation form** to help users navigate the database. A Navigation form has the same purpose as a switchboard, but uses a more familiar Web-like interface and is much easier to create. While Navigation forms are designed for database users, you can customize the Navigation Pane to find and use database objects more easily as you are designing the database. The Access 2010 Navigation Pane now includes a Search text box that you can use to search for database objects.

Apply it in SAM!

- Copy a database object
- Rename a database object
- Delete a database object
- Group objects in the Navigation Pane

Create a form for navigation

1. Click the Create tab on the Ribbon.
2. In the Forms group, click the Navigation button to display a gallery of navigation layouts.

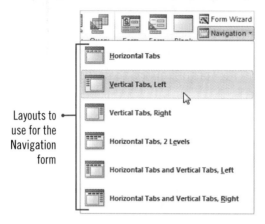

Layouts to use for the Navigation form

3. Click a layout you want to use for the Navigation form.
4. Drag forms and reports from the Navigation Pane to the buttons on the Navigation form.

Copy a database object

1. In the Navigation Pane, right-click the database object you want to copy, such as the Sales Reps table, then click Copy on the shortcut menu.
2. Right-click the group in the Navigation Pane where you want to paste the object, and then click Paste. If you are copying a table, click Structure Only to copy the table design, not the data; click Structure and Data to copy the design and the data; or click Append Data to Existing Table to copy only the data to an existing table.

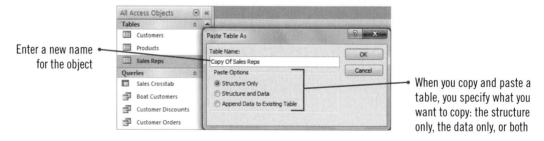

Enter a new name for the object

When you copy and paste a table, you specify what you want to copy: the structure only, the data only, or both

3. Enter a new name for the object, if necessary, then click OK.

Rename a database object

1. In the Navigation Pane, right-click the database object you want to rename, such as the Copy of Sales Reps table, then click Rename on the shortcut menu.

2. Type a new name for the table, such as "Vendors", then click press [Enter].

Delete a database object

1. In the Navigation Pane, click the database object you want to delete.

2. Press [Delete]. A dialog box opens asking you to confirm the deletion.

3. Click Yes. If you are deleting a table that is part of a relationship, a dialog box opens explaining that you must delete the relationships before deleting the table.

QUICK TIP
When you delete a table, you delete all references to it in queries and reports.

Group objects in the Navigation Pane

1. Click the bar at the top of the Navigation Pane to display the Navigation menu.
   - To change the category, click an option in the Navigate To Category section.
   - To change the group, click an option in the Filter By Group section.

2. If you need to create a custom group, right-click the bar at the top of the Navigation Pane, click Navigation Options, click Custom or a custom group, click Add Group, enter a name for the new group, press [Enter], then click OK.

3. To add an unassigned object to a group in the Navigation Pane, display the group to which you want to add an object, then drag the object to the group.

QUICK TIP
The default category is Tables and Related Views, which arranges objects by tables, and the default group is All Tables, which shows all the tables in the database.

Access 2010

Find objects in the database

1. To search the entire database for an object, select a predefined category in the Navigation Pane. Access searches for objects only in the categories and groups displayed in the Navigation Pane.

2. To display the Search text box at the top of the Navigation Pane, right-click the bar at the top of the Navigation Pane, then click Search Bar.

3. Start typing the name of the object you want to find, such as Boat Customers. As you type, Access searches for objects with names that match the text you are typing and displays them in the Navigation Pane.

Navigation Pane bar

Text entered in the Search text box

Click to clear the search text

Two objects with names that start with "bo"

Using Access 2010 databases in Access 2007

In general, you can use Access 2010 databases in Access 2007, though not all the objects and features are available. When you use Access 2007 to open an Access 2010 database that contains certain upgraded features, such as data macros and calculated fields, a Compatibility Warning bar appears below the Ribbon. You can click the More Info button to learn how Access 2007 will handle the Access 2010 features. For example, Access 2007 cannot display Web Browser controls and Navigation forms.

⚠ **Compatibility Warning**   This database uses some features which may be incompatible with the current version of Microsoft Office Access.   More Info ...

Perform repetitive tasks with macros

In Access 2010, you can use the revamped **Macro Designer** to quickly create and edit macros that automate programming tasks such as opening and closing forms and running reports. Access 2010 features many new macro actions you can use to build more powerful macros than in earlier versions of Access. For example, you can now handle errors gracefully by using new error-handling macro actions, which were previously available only by coding in Visual Basic for Applications (VBA). Use the new **data macros** to validate and ensure the accuracy of data whenever you add, update, or delete data in a table. You can create two types of data macros—**event-driven data macros**, which are triggered by table events, and **named data macros**, which run when they are called by name.

Create a macro

1. Click the Create tab on the Ribbon.

2. In the Macros & Code group, click the Macro button. The Macro Designer opens.

3. To add an action to the macro, click the Add New Action arrow button, then select an action from the list, such as OpenForm, or expand a folder in the Action Catalog, if necessary, then double-click an action. Options related to the action you selected appear in the Macro Designer.

4. Select parameters, arguments, and other options for the macro action. For example, enter the name of the form you want the OpenForm action to open.

> **QUICK TIP**
>
> You can also drag a macro action from the Action Catalog to the Macro Designer to insert a new action between two existing actions, for example.

Macro action that opens a form

Macro parameters, such as the name of the form to open

You can also double-click an action in the Action Catalog to add it to your macro

Click to select an action to add to your macro

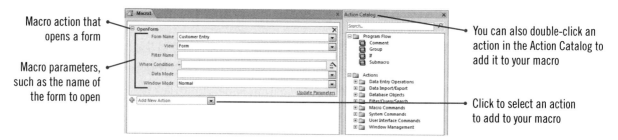

5. Add the other actions you want the macro to perform.

6. Click the Save button 💾 on the Quick Access toolbar, enter a name for the macro, then click OK. The macro is stored in the Macros group of the Navigation Pane.

Create an event-driven data macro

An event-driven data macro runs whenever you add, update, or delete data in a table. You can program a data macro to run immediately after any of these three events, or immediately before a delete or update event.

1. In Design view, open the table to which you want to add the data macro.

2. In the Field, Record & Table Events group, click the Create Data Macros button to display a list of table events.

3. Click the table event you want to trigger the macro. For example, to create a data macro that runs after you update a record in the table, click After Update.

Table open in Design view →

Create Data Macros button

Table events

4. In the Macro Designer, add the actions you want the macro to perform.

Macro uses the If function to add logic to the table

When the CampaignStatus field value is Complete, then the PercentComplete field is updated to display 1, or 100%

Expand categories as necessary in the Action Catalog

- Double-click the If function in the Program Flow folder in the Action Catalog.
- Type the criteria for the If function, [CampaignStatus]="Complete", then press [Enter].
- Double-click the Edit Record block in the Data Blocks folder in the Action Catalog, then double-click the Set Field action in the Data Actions folder.
- Enter PercentComplete as the name of the field, and enter 1 as the value to set.

5. Save and close the data macro.

Create a named data macro

You create a named data macro for a table, but you don't associate it with an event. Instead, you run a named data macro by calling it from any other macro.

1. In Design view, open the table to which you want to add the named data macro.

2. In the Field, Record, & Table Events group, click the Create Data Macros button, then click Create Named Macro. The Macro Designer opens.

3. Add the actions for the macro, then save and close the named data macro.

Ideas for Data Macros

use this table event	in the following scenario
After Insert	After inserting a new Order record, create and send an e-mail notifying a customer that you received their order
After Update	After updating a Payment Status field to set it to *Paid*, update the Balance Due field to $0
After Delete	After deleting a customer record, add a record to the Customer Stats table to keep track of past customers
Before Delete	Before deleting a record in the Payments table, copy the record to the Audits table to keep track of payments
Before Change	Before changing a Donations table to add a new pledge, make sure the contributor has paid any outstanding pledges

Access 2010

Publish databases on the Web

Because the Web is the new desktop for many people and businesses, Access 2010 provides a Web-ready format for databases. In previous versions of Access, you could publish to the Web using scripting technologies to access the data. Now you can simply create and publish Web databases using Backstage view and Access Services, a new component of SharePoint. You build and maintain the database in Access 2010, and users interact with the data using their Web browser. This keeps your data secure, helps you share data throughout an organization or over the Internet, and lets you create database applications that don't require users to have Access. Web databases cannot include some features of desktop databases. Some are listed in the "Where a Web Database Stores and Runs Objects" table. See Access Help for complete details.

Create a Web database

1. On the Ribbon, click the File tab to open Backstage view.

2. On the Navigation bar, click New.

    - To create a Web database from scratch, click the Blank web database button, click the Browse folder button 📁, navigate to where you want to store your database, type a name in the File name text box, click OK, then click the Create button.

    - To create a Web database based on a template, click Sample templates, click the Web database template you want to use for the new database, then click Create.

3. Create tables and other objects in the database as you normally would.

4. To set the Navigation form or any other form to open when the Web database opens, click the File tab, click Options to open the Access Options dialog box, click Current Database, click the Web Display Form list arrow, then select the form you want to open as the default Web display form.

> **QUICK TIP**
> In a Web database, you can design forms and reports only in Layout view.

> **QUICK TIP**
> A Web database does not display the Navigation Pane when it's published on the Web, so one of your first tasks should be to create a Navigation form.

Main form for navigating the Web database

Tabs for opening Web database objects

Publish a database on the Web

You need to have an account on a SharePoint site to publish your Web database from Access 2010. Make sure you know the Web address of the SharePoint server where you want to publish the database.

1. On the Ribbon, click the File tab to open Backstage view.

2. To find out whether any objects, settings, or other content in your database will not appear on the Web, click the Save & Publish tab, then click Publish to Access Services to display the Access Services Overview in the right pane.

Publish to Access Services on the Share tab

Click the Run Compatibility Checker button to identify items and settings that are not supported on the Web

3. Click the Run Compatibility Checker button. If Access finds compatibility problems, click the Web Compatibility Issues button to learn more about them.

4. When you're ready to publish the database, click the Server URL text box, enter the Web address of the SharePoint server where you will publish the database, click the Site Name text box, then enter the name of the Web database.

QUICK TIP

If you want to publish a Web database without running the Compatibility Checker, click the File tab, then click the Publish to Access Services button on the Info tab.

This button is active only if your Web database has compatibility issues

Enter server and site information

5. Click the Publish to Access Services button.

Synchronize design changes

After you make design changes to a database or work with it offline, you need to synchronize the database. Synchronizing resolves differences between the database file on your computer and the SharePoint site.

1. In Access 2010, open the Web database you want to synchronize.

2. On the Ribbon, click the File tab, then click Info, if necessary.

3. Click the Sync All button. (This button appears only if you need to synchronize.)

Where a Web Database Stores and Runs Objects

object/view	runs in a browser	runs on the server	stored in a SharePoint list	not included
Data			√	
Data macro		√		
Design view				√
Form	√			
Group functions				√
Macro	√			√
Navigation Pane				√
Query		√		
Report	√			
Switchboard				√
VBA				√

Using Access 2010 and SharePoint 2010

When you publish a Web database, Access Services creates a SharePoint site that contains the database. All of the compatible database objects and data move to SharePoint lists in that site. SharePoint visitors can use your database according to the permissions they have for accessing the SharePoint site. Visitors with Full Control can change the data and the database design. Visitors with Contribute control can change the data, but not the design. Those with Read control can read the data, but they can't change anything.

Access 2010

Explore other Access improvements

In addition to what you've already explored, Access 2010 offers other new features and improvements. To help you visualize and compare data, Access reports can now display **data bars**. You can also create a **Multiple Items form** that displays more than one record on the form. In previous versions of Access, you could install an add-in to export data to a Portable Document Format (PDF) or an XML Paper Specification (XPS) file format. This feature is now built into Access 2010. Export a form, report, or datasheet to a .pdf file or an .xps file when you want to distribute formatted information people can view without installing Access. You can also connect to a Web service such as one that provides updated stock market information, and use that Web service as a data source.

Display data bars in a report

1. Open a report in Layout view or Design view, then click the field where you want to display data bars.

2. Click the Report Layout Tools Format tab, if necessary, then click the Conditional Formatting button in the Control Formatting group. The Conditional Formatting Rules Manager dialog box opens.

3. Click the New Rule button to open the New Formatting Rule dialog box.

4. In the Select a rule type section, click Compare to other records to display the data bar format settings.

5. To show data bars that compare values, click the Shortest Bar list arrow, then click a type. Click the Longest bar list arrow, then click a type.

6. Click the Bar color list arrow, then select a color.

7. Click OK to close the New Formatting Rule dialog box, enter requested values, if necessary, then click OK to display the data bars in the report.

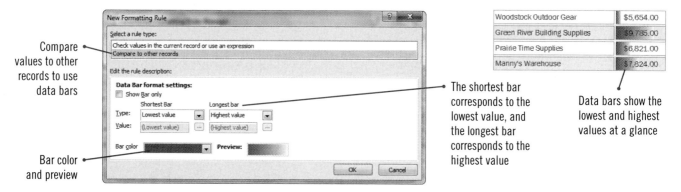

Compare values to other records to use data bars

Bar color and preview

The shortest bar corresponds to the lowest value, and the longest bar corresponds to the highest value

Data bars show the lowest and highest values at a glance

Create a Multiple Items form

1. In the Navigation Pane, click the table or query that contains the data you want to include in the form.

2. Click the Create tab, then click the More Forms button in the Forms group.

3. Click Multiple Items.

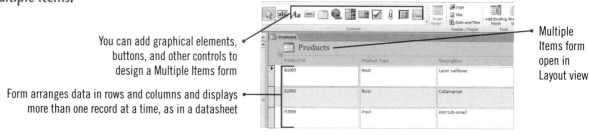

You can add graphical elements, buttons, and other controls to design a Multiple Items form

Form arranges data in rows and columns and displays more than one record at a time, as in a datasheet

Multiple Items form open in Layout view

Export to PDF and XPS

1. Open the object you want to export to a PDF or XPS file.

2. On the Ribbon, click the File tab to open Backstage view, then click Save & Publish on the Navigation bar.

3. In the File Types list, click Save Object As, click PDF or XPS, then click the Save As button. The Publish as PDF or XPS dialog box opens.

4. Navigate to where you want to create the file, enter a name for the file, if necessary, then select whether you want to optimize for standard publishing or minimum size publishing.

5. Click the Publish button. The object opens as a PDF or XPS file.

Products form published as a PDF file

Work confidently with updated security features

Access 2010 enhances Access 2007 security features by integrating with Microsoft SharePoint Foundation 2010. This service lets you keep track of database revisions, set access permissions, and recover deleted data. Access 2010 also streamlines the way you open databases:

- To enable a database not stored in a trusted location, you can now click Enable Content on the Security Warning bar instead of opening a dialog box.

- You do not need to enable content when you open a recently opened database (those listed on the Recent page in Backstage view).

Get Help

1. On the Ribbon, click the File tab to open Backstage view.

2. Click Help on the Navigation bar.

3. Click an option in the Support section, such as Microsoft Office Help.

Validating fields in Access 2010

If you're designing a database, you want to make sure people enter valid data that makes sense in the database. For example, suppose your Orders table includes a Status field where you enter 1 for an active order, 2 for a delayed order, and 3 for a completed order. To make sure users enter only 1, 2, or 3, you can set a field validation rule for the Status field. In Access 2010, you can create the rule in Datasheet view as you're setting up the table or entering data. In the Field Validation group on the Table Tools Fields tab, click the Validation button, click Field Validation Rule, then enter the rule, such as <3. You use the simplified Expression Builder to enter the rule, which streamlines the process of entering expressions.

Access 2010

Access 2010 Quick Reference

To Do This	Go Here	To Do This	Go Here
Add field in Datasheet view	Click to Add column heading | Click data type *or* Table Tools Fields tab | More Fields button | Click data type	Create database from template	File tab | New | Sample templates
Add Navigation control to form	Form Design Tools Design tab | Controls More button | Navigation Control	Create field with data type	Datasheet view | Click the Click to Add column heading *or* Datasheet view | Table Tools Fields tab | Add & Delete group | More Fields button
Add related fields in Datasheet view	Table Tools Fields tab | Add & Delete group | More Fields button | Click Quick Start field	Create Navigation form	Create tab | Forms group | Navigation button | Navigation layout
Add Web Browser control to form	Form Design Tools Design tab | Controls More button | Web Browser Control	Create table from application part	Create tab | Templates group | Applications Parts button | Quick Start table
Apply Office theme	Design tab for form or report | Themes group | Themes button	Create table in Datasheet view	Create tab | Tables group |Table button
Back up database	File tab | Save & Publish | Back Up Database, Save As button	Create Web database	File tab | New | Blank web database
Change data type of field in Datasheet view	Click field value | Table Tools Fields tab | Formatting group | Data Type arrow button	Display data bars in a report	Report Layout (or Design) Tools Format tab | Control Formatting group | Conditional Formatting button | New Rule
Compact and repair database	File tab | Info | Compact & Repair Database button	Enable database	Enable Content button
Create a calculated field	Table Design view | Data Type arrow | Calculated	Enter expression with Expression Builder	Table Design view | Data Type arrow | Calculated
Create a field validation rule	Datasheet view | Table Tools Fields tab | Field Validation group | Validation button | Field Validation Rule	Export to PDF and XPS	File tab | Save & Publish | Save Object As | PDF or XPS
Create a form with the Form Wizard	Create tab | Forms group | Form Wizard button	Open database	File tab | Open
Create a macro	Create tab | Macros & Code group | Macro button | Add New Action list arrow	Open recent database	File tab | Recent
Create a Multiple Item form	Table or query in Navigation Pane | Create tab | Forms group | More Forms button | Multiple Items	Print report	File tab | Print | Quick Print *or* File tab | Print | Print | Choose print settings | OK
Create a named data macro	Table Design view | Field, Record, & Table Events group | Create Data Macros button | Create Named Macro | Macro actions	Publish Web database	File tab | Info | Publish to Access Services button
Create an event-driven data macro	Table Design view | Fields, Record, & Table Events group | Create Data Macros button | Table event | Macro actions	Search in Navigation Pane	Right-click Navigation Pane bar | Search Bar
Create blank database	File tab | New | Blank database	Synchronize Web database	File tab | Info | Sync All button

4 Upgrading to PowerPoint 2010

The wealth of features in PowerPoint 2010 will shift your presentations into multimedia overdrive. You can apply artistic effects to photos and apply complex animations to multiple objects. Moving into more powerful territory, you can now embed and trim video, and then apply a style to it. PowerPoint 2010 also makes it easier to save and share your presentations for nearly any delivery platform. The Office button has been replaced by the File tab, where you can use Backstage view for common file, print, and template commands, and tap into new sharing options. Once you get up to speed on the new features, creating high-impact presentations will be an efficient process. ■■■■ As you review these lessons, you will be able to practice many of the skills using Skills Assessment Manager (SAM). The lessons will cover SAM skills and tasks as outlined in this table.

Lesson	SAM Tasks	
Manage files in Backstage view	■ Create a new presentation from a template ■ Open an existing presentation ■ Print speaker notes	■ Save a presentation ■ Close a presentation ■ Exit PowerPoint
Adjust a photo	■ Apply an effect to an image	■ Insert a SmartArt graphic
Apply slide transitions	■ Apply transition effects to a single slide	
Add and modify animation	■ Apply an entrance animation effect to a shape ■ Animate a shape using a motion path	■ Use the Animation Painter
Work with video	■ Insert video in a slide	■ Trim an inserted video
Use advanced video effects	■ Apply an effect to a video	■ Add a trigger to media
Share a slideshow	■ Record a slide show as a video	■ Broadcast a slide show
Manage large presentations	■ Insert a section into a slide show	■ Compress media

Manage files in Backstage view

Clicking the File tab opens Backstage view, where you can create a new presentation, and access all the features and actions that affect and impact an existing presentation. Here you can open, save, and close presentations, and exit the program. You can also manage files, print, and send your presentation.

Create a new presentation from a template

1. Click the File tab on the Ribbon to open Backstage view. By default, the Info tab is in front. It displays information about the current document, including properties and author information.

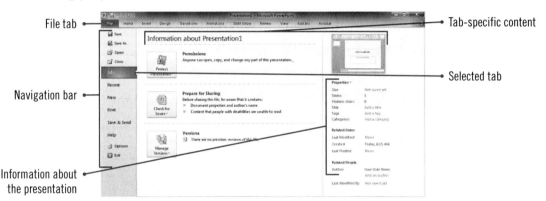

File tab • — • Tab-specific content

• Selected tab

Navigation bar •

Information about • the presentation

2. Click New on the Navigation bar. The themes and templates that are available on your computer or at Office.com appear in the center pane.

3. Click a template category, such as Sample templates, then click a template icon to view a larger thumbnail in the Preview pane. Many templates have animation, transitions, and effects already built in.

QUICK TIP
You can also create a new a presentation using commands on the Quick Access toolbar.

Navigate using the Back, Forward, and Home buttons

New tab •

Thumbnail previews • of templates

• Preview pane

• Click here to create a new presentation based on the selected template

Current category is Sample templates

4. To create a new presentation based on a template, click the Create button in the right pane, or double-click an icon. To use a presentation created from a template, you just substitute your own content in the slides.

QUICK TIP
To return to main Backstage view, click the Home button 🏠 at the top of the center pane.

Open an existing presentation

1. Click the File tab on the Ribbon to open Backstage view. Recently opened presentations appear on the Recent tab; click to open in PowerPoint.

If you don't see the presentation you want to open, click to open the Open dialog box

Click to open a recent presentation

Recent tab

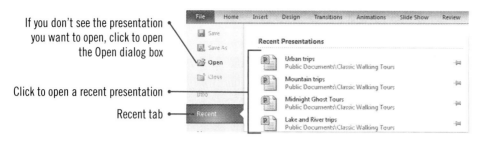

Print a presentation

1. Click the File tab on the Ribbon to open Backstage view, then click Print on the Navigation bar. Choices for the printer and options for what to print appear in the center pane.

2. Click the Full Page Slides button list arrow, then click the item you want to print—for example, Notes Pages.

Print button

Print tab

Click to choose what to print

Click a print layout option

Preview of current slide and notes

Notes Pages

3. When you've selected and previewed the print job, click the Print button.

Save and close a presentation and exit PowerPoint

1. Click the File tab on the Ribbon to open Backstage view.

2. Click Save on the Navigation bar. The presentation is saved, and Backstage view closes.

3. Click the File tab on the Ribbon, then click Close on the Navigation bar. The presentation closes, and the workspace is blank.

4. If you are finished working in PowerPoint, click the File tab on the Ribbon, then click Exit on the Navigation bar. PowerPoint closes.

PowerPoint 2010

Adjust a photo

PowerPoint 2010 contains substantive photo-editing features that give you more creative control over the appearance of your photographs. **Artistic effects** emulate painting, sketching, or drawing styles, and can highlight or complement design elements in your presentation. The Remove Background feature in PowerPoint 2010 allows you to remove solid color and determine which areas of the selection you want to keep or discard. You can also use SmartArt graphics to transform photos into striking visuals.

Apply an artistic effect to a photo

1. Select a photo in a slide, then click Artistic Effects in the Adjust group on the Picture Tools Format tab.

2. Move the mouse pointer over each effect to preview it live in the picture.

QUICK TIP

When applying an artistic effect, you can select only one photo at a time and apply only one effect to it.

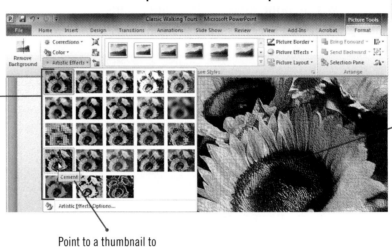

Thumbnail previews of each effect appear here

Live preview of effect in slide

Point to a thumbnail to view the effect's name

3. Click an effect to apply it to the photo.

Remove the background in a photo

1. Click a photo in a slide, then click the Remove Background button in the Adjust group on the Picture Tools Format tab. A marquee indicates the default selection for which areas to keep and which to remove. The magenta area is the background of the photo that PowerPoint initially selects for removal.

Selections in original color will be retained

Marquee surrounds area containing selections to be retained; move or resize to change selections

Areas highlighted in magenta will be removed

2. Use the buttons in the Refine group on the Background Removal tab to customize the area you want to remove.

QUICK TIP
Before using the Mark Areas to Keep and the Mark Areas to Remove buttons, you can move and resize the marquee to make a different selection.

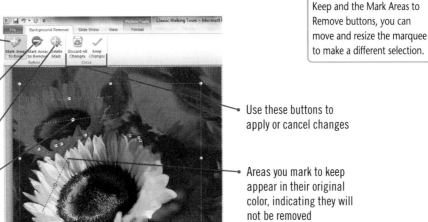

Click this button, then click any magenta areas to mark points, or click and drag to mark larger areas

Click this button, then click any areas to mark for removal

Click this button, then click to delete any markers

Areas you mark to remove appear highlighted in magenta, indicating they will be removed

Use these buttons to apply or cancel changes

Areas you mark to keep appear in their original color, indicating they will not be removed

3. Click the Keep Changes button in the Close group to apply the changes or the Discard All Changes button to cancel the background removal and leave the photo unchanged.

The slide background theme color is visible after background of the photo is removed

Add pictures to a SmartArt graphic

1. Click the slide where you want to insert a SmartArt graphic, click the Insert tab on the Ribbon, then click SmartArt in the Illustrations group.
2. In the Choose a SmartArt graphic dialog box, click the Picture category, click a graphic, then click OK.
3. In the SmartArt graphic, click the placeholder you want to fill.

Click to insert text

Click to insert a photo

Inserted photo

Inserted text

4. Navigate to the location where you store your photos, select the photo, then click Open in the Insert Picture dialog box.
5. Click a text placeholder to add text. When you are finished adding photos and text, click a blank area of the slide to deselect the SmartArt.

PowerPoint 2010

Apply slide transitions

PowerPoint 2010 offers more choices for applying and working with slide transitions. You can access a range of different transition effects on the Transitions tab. You'll notice that transitions are much more energized and smoother, and better organized to help you determine which effect is best for your content. New to PowerPoint 2010 are transitions that affect only the content on a slide, while preserving the slide's background and theme as a static image. With most transitions, the new slide appears after the transition is displayed. However, if the new slide includes any animated content, a new blank slide appears first and then animated content in the slide plays.

Apply a slide transition to a slide

1. Click a slide, click the Transitions tab on the Ribbon, then point to a transition in the Transition to This Slide group to preview it on the slide.

2. Click a transition to apply it to the slide. The transition plays again when you click it.

QUICK TIP
To apply the transition to multiple slides at once, select two or more slides prior to clicking a transition.

Click to preview transition after applying it to a slide

Transitions tab

Click a transition to apply it

Click to view more transitions

Glitter transition in progress

3. To preview a transition you've applied, select the slide, then click the Preview button in the Preview group on the Transitions tab.

QUICK TIP
Click the More button  to view the entire gallery.

Editing a PowerPoint 2010 presentation in older versions of PowerPoint

PowerPoint 2007 and 2010 share the common .pptx file extension, and you can open PowerPoint 2010 files in PowerPoint 2007. However, they do not share backward compatibility in all features. If you edit a 2010 file in PowerPoint 2007 you do not retain the 2010 functionality. When you open a 2010 presentation in 2007, you lose any transition and animation effects or other features not available in PowerPoint 2007. Unsupported transition effects default to a Fade effect.

Modify a slide transition

1. Select one or more slides containing a transition, then click the Transitions tab on the Ribbon.

2. Click the Effect Options button in the Transition to This Slide group, then click a direction or shape option. The options available vary depending on the transition you have applied. In this case, we've started with a Fly Through transition, so we have four options to choose from.

By default, the transition is applied to selected slide only

To apply transitions to multiple slides, first select them in the Slides tab

Currently selected transition

Click to choose an effect option for selected transition

Options for selected transition

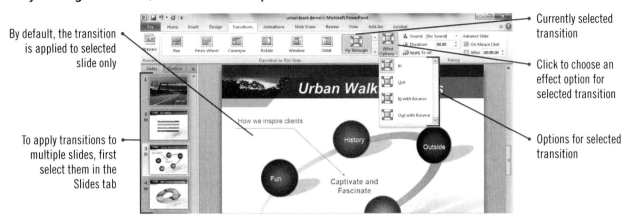

3. Use the settings in the Timing group to customize additional settings.

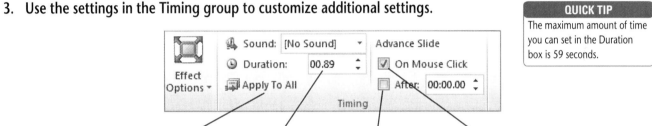

Click to apply transition or timing changes to all slides

Adjust to lengthen or shorten the time the transition plays

Click to add a check mark, then set the delay time before the transition advances to the next slide

Leave selected if you want to manually click the mouse to advance to the next slide

4. Click the Slide Show button 🖥 on the status bar to preview the transitions and timing in the slides.

PowerPoint 2010

Add and modify animation

Animation is powered in a new way in PowerPoint 2010, and the difference to users is dramatic: sleek and smooth motion. It's easier to add multiple animations to an object. You can adjust how fast an object starts and stops in a slide, so you can create more organic movement or just a great effect. Best of all, once you've tweaked the settings for one or more animations, you can use the **Animation Painter** to transfer the animation and its custom settings to any other object in any open presentation. Some features, such as motion paths, were available in PowerPoint 2007, but they are much easier to access in 2010. Now you can easily use a motion path to create unique movement in a slide.

Apply it in SAM!
- Apply an entrance animation effect to a shape
- Animate a shape using a motion path
- Use the Animation Painter

Add animation to an object

1. Select the object in a slide you want to apply an animation to, then click the Animations tab on the Ribbon.

2. Preview the animations in the Animation group, then click an animation to apply it to the selected object. To replace the animation, just click another animation in the gallery.

QUICK TIP
Click the More button ▼ to view the entire gallery.

Click to preview animation in the current slide

Selected animation is highlighted in gallery

Click to add multiple animations to an object

Animation selected by its tag number

3. To add additional animations or customize the effect, use the commands in the Advanced Animation group. You can click the Add Animation button, then click an animation to add additional animations to the object.

4. Click the Preview button in the Preview group to view all your changes to the object at once.

QUICK TIP
To see which animation is applied to an object, click the numbered animation tag next to an object on the slide to select it; PowerPoint highlights the applicable icon in the Animation gallery.

Adjusting the entry and finish speed of an animation

You can adjust an object's acceleration and deceleration using controls on the Effect tab of any animation dialog box. To do so, display the Animation pane by clicking the Animation pane button in the Advanced Animation group, right-click the animation in the Animation pane, then click Effect Options. The dialog box specific to the animation opens. Here you can drag the Smooth start slider to speed up the start motion, and you can drag the Smooth end slider to speed up the end motion. You can also add a bounce, but only if the Smooth end value is zero. Note that not all animations include all options.

Drag sliders to change motion speed or add a bounce

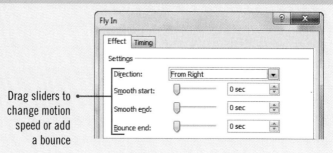

Use the Animation Painter

1. Click an animated object in the slide, then click the Animation Painter button in the Advanced Animation group.

2. Click another object in the slide. The animation and its attributes are transferred, or "painted," to the object.

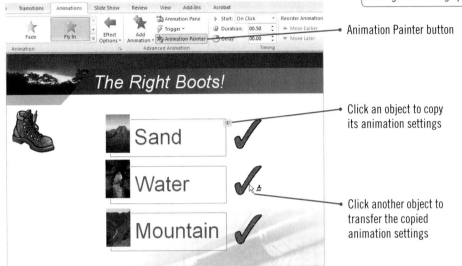

Animation Painter button

Click an object to copy its animation settings

Click another object to transfer the copied animation settings

3. Click the Preview button in the Preview group to view all animation effects in the current slide.

Add and adjust a motion path

1. Click an object in a slide, then click either the More button ⬇ in the Animation group or the Add Animation button in the Advanced Animation group. Scroll down, then click a motion path in the Motions Paths category.

2. Drag the start or end handles to change the where the motion path begins or ends, or drag a sizing handle to increase or decrease the length or shape of the motion path.

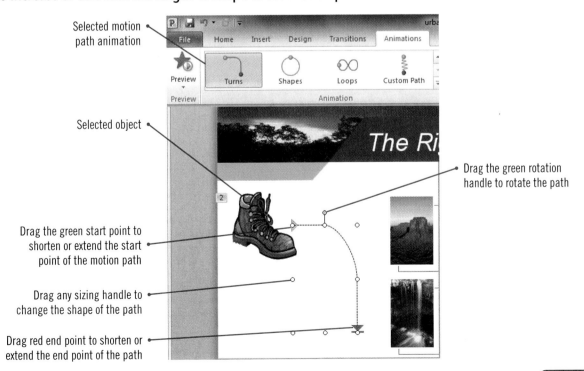

Selected motion path animation

Selected object

Drag the green start point to shorten or extend the start point of the motion path

Drag any sizing handle to change the shape of the path

Drag red end point to shorten or extend the end point of the path

Drag the green rotation handle to rotate the path

Work with video

Video is a rich experience in PowerPoint 2010. For a start, you can embed or link video as easily as you can insert a still image. You can then edit it right from within PowerPoint to create the perfect visual event for your viewers. You can use features on the Video Tools Format tab to correct brightness and contrast in a video, or to colorize it. You can edit the length and start/end points using the **Trim** feature on the Video Tools Playback tab, or set the video to fade in or out or to play full screen. You can also select a **poster frame**, a still image created from a frame of the video to serve as the video's "cover" or preview image on the slide.

Insert a video in a slide

1. Click the slide where you want the video to appear, click the Insert tab on the Ribbon, then click the Video button list arrow in the Media group.

2. Choose how you want to insert your video.

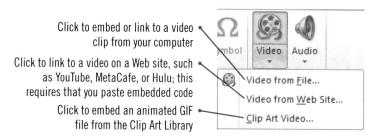

Click to embed or link to a video clip from your computer

Click to link to a video on a Web site, such as YouTube, MetaCafe, or Hulu; this requires that you paste embedded code

Click to embed an animated GIF file from the Clip Art Library

Video from File...
Video from Web Site...
Clip Art Video...

QUICK TIP
To insert a video from a Web site, navigate to the Web site, click the Embed link or text box, copy the embed code, then return to PowerPoint and paste the code in the Insert Video from Web Site dialog box, when prompted.

3. Use the commands on the Video Tools Format tab to customize how the video looks and plays on the slide.

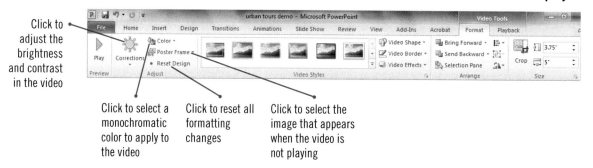

Click to adjust the brightness and contrast in the video

Click to select a monochromatic color to apply to the video

Click to reset all formatting changes

Click to select the image that appears when the video is not playing

4. Use the playback controls to watch the video, and use commands on the Video Tools Playback tab to customize how the video behaves within the presentation.

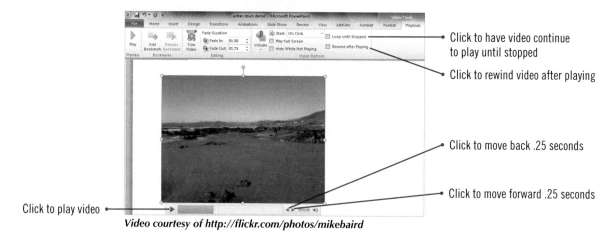

Click to have video continue to play until stopped

Click to rewind video after playing

Click to move back .25 seconds

Click to move forward .25 seconds

Click to play video

Video courtesy of http://flickr.com/photos/mikebaird

Trim an inserted video

1. Select an inserted video in a slide, click the Video Tools Playback tab on the Ribbon, then click the Trim Video button in the Editing group. The Trim Video dialog box opens, where you can drag markers to create new start and end times.

2. Use the controls in the Trim Video dialog box trim the video.

Click to open Trim Video controls

Click to adjust how long the video fades in and out

Drag green start point to a new start frame

Drag red end point to a new end frame

If the video contains sound, you can use the audio graph to locate exact frame to trim

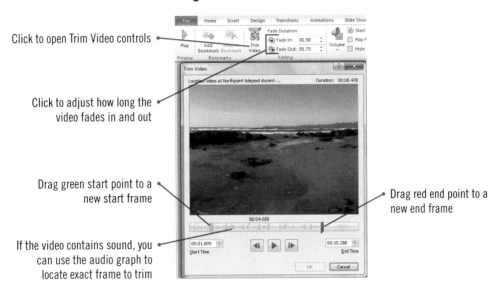

3. Click OK to close the Trim Video dialog box, then play the video to view the new start and end times.

Select a poster frame

1. Click to select the video on the slide.

2. If you want to use a frame of the video as a poster frame, play the video, then pause it when you see a frame you want to use as the poster frame. Click the Video Tools Format tab on the Ribbon, click the Poster Frame button in the Adjust group, then click Current Frame.

QUICK TIP
PowerPoint automatically resizes the image you select to fit in the video frame.

Click to select the current frame as the poster frame

Click to select a file on your computer as the poster frame

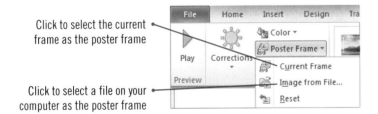

3. To test the poster frame, play the video, pause it, then click another area of the slide. The poster image appears whenever the video is not playing.

QUICK TIP
To use an image as a poster frame, select the video, click the Video Tools Format tab, click the Poster Frame button, click Image from File, navigate to where the image is stored, click the image, then click Insert.

Use advanced video effects

Inserting a video into your presentation is just the first step in delivering more action in your presentations. You can format your video using many of the features you're familiar with when formatting other objects. Add a frame with a simple border, apply an engaging style, or add effects, such as shadows, reflections, and glows. You can even transform the appearance of your video into a shape, such as a heart or a thought bubble. You can extend the multimedia impact of video by adding a **bookmark** to mark the frame where you want to trim a video, or to identify other specific frames of interest. You can also use a bookmark to trigger another action in your video, such as jumping to a particular frame, displaying text or a shape, or playing a sound or another video.

Add a style to a video

1. Select an inserted video in a slide, click the Video Tools Format tab on the Ribbon if necessary, then click a style in the Video Style group.

Click a style to apply it

Click to open gallery of all styles

2. Customize the style by applying a shape, border, or effect, or any combination you choose.

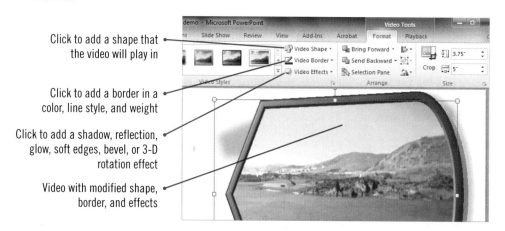

Click to add a shape that the video will play in

Click to add a border in a color, line style, and weight

Click to add a shadow, reflection, glow, soft edges, bevel, or 3-D rotation effect

Video with modified shape, border, and effects

Add a bookmark to a video

1. Play a video, then click the Pause button ▐▐ in the playback controls when you reach the frame you want to bookmark.

2. Click the Video Tools Playback tab on the Ribbon, then click the Add Bookmark button in the Bookmarks group.

Click to add a bookmark

3. When playing the video, double-click the bookmark, which appears as yellow dot on the playback control timeline, to move to its location in the video. You can use this bookmark to trigger an event, such as animation that causes an object to appear at a certain point.

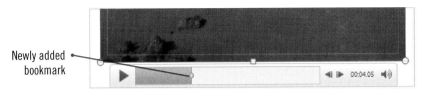

Newly added bookmark

Add a trigger to media

1. Select the video in the slide that contains a bookmark; or, if necessary, add a bookmark at the location where you want to trigger an event.

2. Click the Insert tab on the Ribbon, then select the object (text, sound, video, clip art, or shape) that will be acted upon when the video reaches the bookmark. The video returns to the poster frame, if one is set.

3. Insert the object in the video where you want it to appear as the video plays. For example, here we want an arrow to fade in on the right when the video reaches the bookmark, but you can select and animate any object or media.

4. Apply the event or action you want to happen. For example, in this case we want an animation that causes the arrow to fade in. To do that, you click the object, click the Animations tab, then click Fade animation in the Animation group.

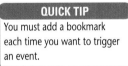

QUICK TIP
You must add a bookmark each time you want to trigger an event.

5. Double-click the bookmark on the playback controls, make sure the object is selected in the slide, click the Trigger button in the Advanced Animation group, click On Bookmark, then locate the bookmark in the list that corresponds to the event. In our example, the bookmark will trigger the animation to play, making the arrow fade in.

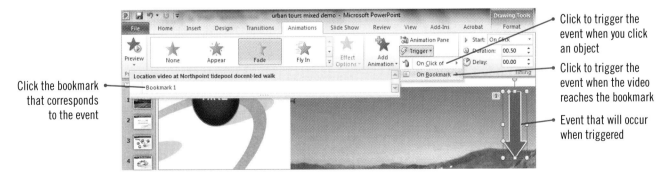

Click the bookmark that corresponds to the event

Click to trigger the event when you click an object

Click to trigger the event when the video reaches the bookmark

Event that will occur when triggered

6. Click the bookmark in the list to synchronize the event to the video. A lightning bolt replaces the event number.

7. To experience the triggered event, you need to view the slide in Slide Show view. Click the Slide Show tab on the Ribbon, then click the From Current Slide button to preview the video.

Share a slide show

PowerPoint 2010 provides many avenues for delivering your presentation to your viewers. Viewers just need a free Windows Live ID to be able to experience your presentation online as you give it—just as if you were in the same room. You can also save your presentation as a video, so viewers can watch it at their convenience.

Record a slide show as a video

1. Click the File tab on the Ribbon to open Backstage view, then click Save & Send.

2. Click Create a Video under File Types in the center pane. Options for creating a video appear in the right pane.

3. Click the Computer & HD Displays arrow, then click an option.

Creates a video with high quality and largest file size

Creates a video with moderate quality and medium file size

Creates a video with low quality and smallest file size

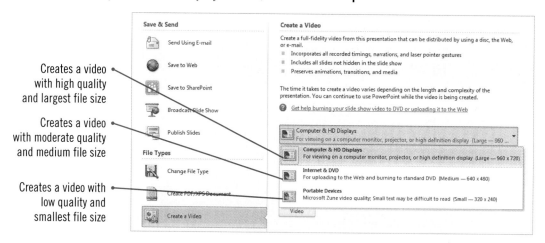

4. Click the Create Video button.

Selected options

Click to save video

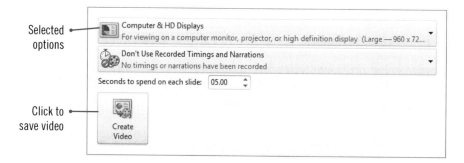

5. Navigate to where you want to store the video, then click Save. PowerPoint creates a .wmv video file that anyone can view in Windows Media Player.

Broadcast a slide show

1. Click the File tab on the Ribbon to open Backstage view, then click Save & Send.

2. Click Broadcast Slide Show under Save & Send in the center pane, then click the Broadcast Slide Show button in the right pane. The Broadcast Slide Show dialog box opens.

Click to start broadcast

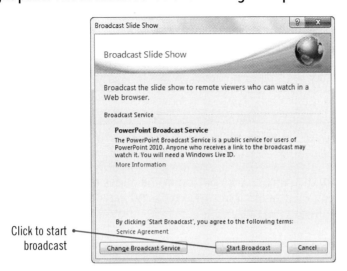

3. Click Start Broadcast, type your Windows Live ID credentials in the Windows Security dialog box, then click OK.

URL of presentation; attendees click this link from an e-mail message

Click to copy URL

Click to send URL to audience

When audience opens URL, click to begin broadcast

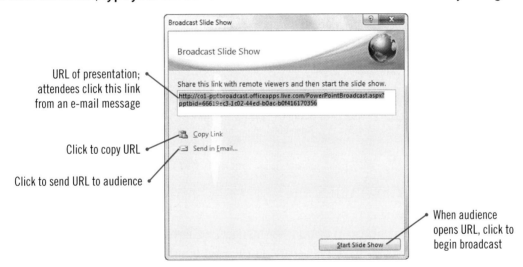

The Broadcast Slide Show dialog box opens, containing a link you send to your remote attendees. You can send this link to up to 50 remote attendees.

4. Click Send in Email to open a new message window, where you can invite people to the broadcast. The e-mail message contains the link to the broadcast. When you've finished adding e-mail addresses, click Send.

QUICK TIP

To exit a broadcast session, press [Esc], then click End Broadcast twice.

Managing large presentations

Long presentations can become difficult to manage, especially if you need to find a particular slide or group of slides quickly, or if several people are working on different slides within it. **Sections** allow you to organize and categorize your presentation to keep things clear. And, if sharing a draft slide show, posting to the Internet, or just trying to balance quality and file size is imperative, PowerPoint 2010 guides you first into optimizing your file, and lets you compress your presentation using the option that best suits your needs.

Insert sections in a slide show

1. In Slide Sorter view or in the Slides tab in Normal view, click between the slides where you want a section to begin.

2. Click the Home tab on the Ribbon, click the Section button in the Slides group, then click Add Section. Here, we added a section in Slide Sorter view. By default, each presentation has a Default Section before the first slide.

> **QUICK TIP**
> You can print and apply effects and themes to an entire section.

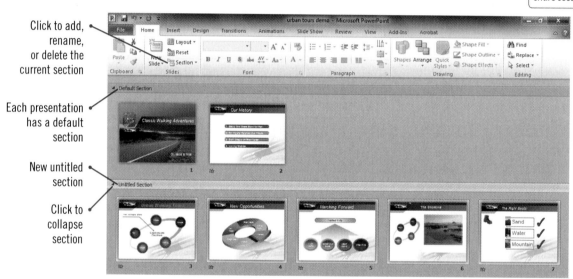

Click to add, rename, or delete the current section

Each presentation has a default section

New untitled section

Click to collapse section

3. Right-click the Untitled Section, then click an option. In this case, we'll rename a section. Click Rename Section, in the Rename Section dialog box, type a name in the Section name text box, then click Rename.

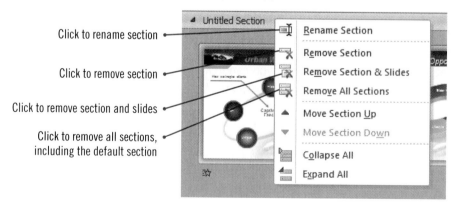

Click to rename section

Click to remove section

Click to remove section and slides

Click to remove all sections, including the default section

Compress media

1. Click the File tab on the Ribbon to open Backstage view, then click Info.

2. Click the Optimize Compatibility Media button in the center pane to optimize and embed media if you've added audio or video and this option is available.

3. Click the Compress Media button, then click an option.

Choose a quality option •————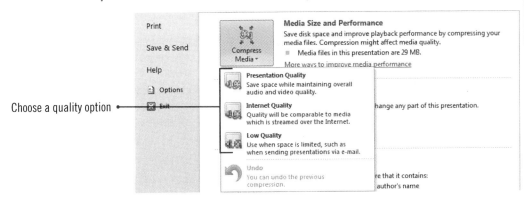

4. Click the Close button when the compression is complete.

Using the Screenshot tool

You can use the Screenshot tool to capture all or part of any open window and insert it in the current slide. Click the Insert tab on the Ribbon, then click the Screenshot button in the Images group. Click an image of an available window to insert the image.

To capture only a portion of an open window, click Screen Clipping, then drag a marquee around the area you want to capture.

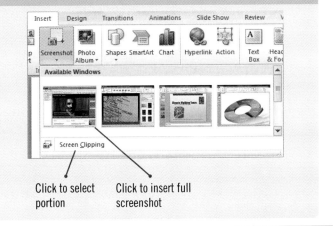

Click to select portion

Click to insert full screenshot

PowerPoint 2010 Quick Reference

To Do This	Go Here	To Do This	Go Here
Add a bookmark	Video Tools Playback tab | Bookmarks group	Customize the Ribbon	File tab | Options | Customize Ribbon
Add a poster frame	Video Tools Format tab | Adjust group	E-mail a presentation as a PDF attachment, or XPS document	File tab | Save & Send
Add a screenshot or screen clipping	Insert tab | Images group | Screenshot button	Improve media size and performance	File tab | Info | Compress Media button
Add a style, border, effect, or layout to a picture	Picture Tools Format tab | Picture Styles group	Insert a Picture SmartArt layout	Insert tab | Illustrations group | SmartArt button
Add a style, shape, border, or effect to a video	Video Tools Format tab | Video Styles group	Insert a video from computer or Web site	Insert tab | Media group | Video button
Add an artistic effect	Picture Tools Format tab | Adjust group	Open a presentation	File tab | Open
Add animation to a slide or object	Animations tab | Advanced Animation group	Open a recent presentation	File tab | Recent
Add, remove, expand, or collapse a section	Home tab | Slides group | Section commands	Optimize media	File tab | Info
Adjust color saturation, tone, and color in a video	Video Tools Format tab | Adjust group | Color button	Package a presentation for a CD and publish slides	File tab | Save & Send
Adjust color saturation, tone, color, and pixels	Picture Tools Format tab | Adjust group	Preview a transition	Transitions tab | Preview group
Adjust the duration of a video fading in and out	Video Tools Playback tab | Editing group	Preview a video	Video Tools Playback or Format tabs | Preview group | Play button
Adjust video options	Video Tools Playback tab	Preview an animation	Animations tab | Preview tab
Apply a transition	Transitions tab | Transition to This Slide group	Protect presentation	File tab | Info
Apply an effect to a transition	Transitions tab | Transition to This Slide group | Effect Options button	Recover draft versions	File tab | Info | Manage Versions button
Apply an effect to an animation	Animations tab | Advanced Animation group | Effect Options button	Recover unsaved presentations	File tab | Recent
Brighten, adjust contrast, soften, or sharpen a photo	Picture Tools Format tab | Adjust group | Corrections button	Rename a section in a presentation	Home tab | Slides group
Broadcast a slide show, change file type	File tab | Save & Send	Save a presentation	File tab | Save or Save As
Close a presentation	File tab | Close	Send a presentation as an Internet fax or to the Web	File tab | Save & Send
Create a new presentation	File tab | New	Set print settings, preview	File tab | Print
Create a PDF/XPS or video	File tab | Save & Send	Trim a video	Video Tools Playback tab | Editing group
Create handouts	File tab | Save & Send	Use the Animation Painter	Animations tab | Advanced Animation group
Crop and resize a video	Video Tools Format tab | Size group		

Working with Windows Live and Office Web Apps

If the computer you are using has an active Internet connection, you can go to the Microsoft Windows Live Web site and access a wide variety of services and Web applications. For example, you can check your e-mail through Windows Live, network with your friends and coworkers, and use your SkyDrive to store and share files. Using Windows Live SkyDrive, you can use Office Web Apps to create and edit Word, PowerPoint, Excel, and OneNote files, even when you are using a computer that does not have Office 2010 installed. ▄▄ ▄ This chapter provides basic information on Windows Live, cloud computing, and Windows Live SkyDrive. It also provides instructions on how to work with an Office Web App, and how to manage and share files on Windows Live SkyDrive. *Note*: The Microsoft Office 2010 Web Apps might be released to consumers after the publication of this book. If you are using this book before the Web Apps are released, then you may not be able to perform all the steps in some of these lessons.

Lessons

Understand Windows Live

Get a Windows Live ID and access your SkyDrive

Upload files to your Windows Live SkyDrive

Work with an Office Web App

Manage files on your Windows Live SkyDrive

Share files on your Windows Live SkyDrive

Understand Windows Live

You can use your Web browser to upload your files to Windows Live from any computer connected to the Internet. You can work on the files right in your Web browser using Office Web Apps and share your files with people in your Windows Live network.

What is Windows Live?

Windows Live is a collection of services and Web applications that you can use to help you be more productive both personally and professionally. For example, you can use Windows Live to send and receive e-mail, to chat with friends via instant messaging, to share photos, to create a blog, and to store and edit files using SkyDrive. Windows Live is a free service that you sign up for. When you sign up, you receive a Windows Live ID. You use your Windows Live ID to sign into Windows Live so you can access Windows Live services, such as SkyDrive and Office Web Apps. When you work with files on Windows Live, you are cloud computing.

What is cloud computing?

The term cloud computing refers to the process of working with files online in a Web browser. When you save files to SkyDrive from Windows Live, you are saving your files to an online location. Windows Live SkyDrive is like having a personal hard drive in the cloud.

What is Windows Live SkyDrive?

Windows Live SkyDrive is an online storage and file-sharing service. With a Windows Live account, you receive access to your own SkyDrive, which is your personal storage area on the Internet. On your SkyDrive, you are given space to store up to 25 GB of data online. Each file can be a maximum size of 50 MB. You can also use your SkyDrive to share files with friends and coworkers. After you upload a file to your SkyDrive, you can choose to make the file visible to the public, to anyone you invite to share your files, or only to yourself. You can also use your SkyDrive to access Office Web Apps, which you use to create and edit files created in Word, OneNote, PowerPoint, and Excel online in your Web browser.

Why use Windows Live SkyDrive?

Windows Live SkyDrive provides you with an additional storage area for your files. You do not have to worry about backing up your files to a personal storage device that could be lost or damaged. Another advantage of storing your files on your SkyDrive is that you can access your files from any computer that has an active Internet connection. The figure below shows the Windows Live SkyDrive Web page that appears when you access it from a Windows Live account. From your SkyDrive, you can also access Office Web Apps.

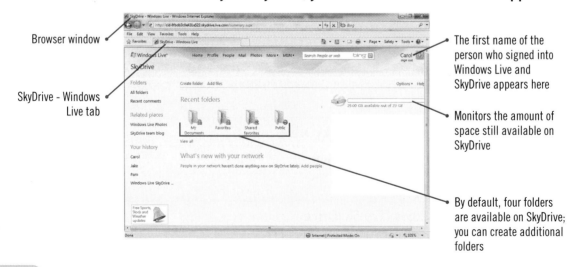

Browser window

SkyDrive - Windows Live tab

The first name of the person who signed into Windows Live and SkyDrive appears here

Monitors the amount of space still available on SkyDrive

By default, four folders are available on SkyDrive; you can create additional folders

What are Office Web Apps?

Office Web Apps are versions of Microsoft Word, Excel, PowerPoint, and OneNote that you can access online from your SkyDrive. An Office Web App does not include all of the features and functions included with the full Office version of its associated application. However, you can use the Office Web App from any computer that is connected to the Internet, even if Microsoft Office 2010 is not installed on that computer.

How do Windows Live SkyDrive and Office Web Apps work together?

You can create a file in Office 2010 using Word, Excel, PowerPoint, or OneNote and then upload the file to your SkyDrive. You can then open the Office file saved to SkyDrive and edit it using your Web browser and the corresponding Office Web App. The figure below shows a PowerPoint presentation open in the PowerPoint Web App.

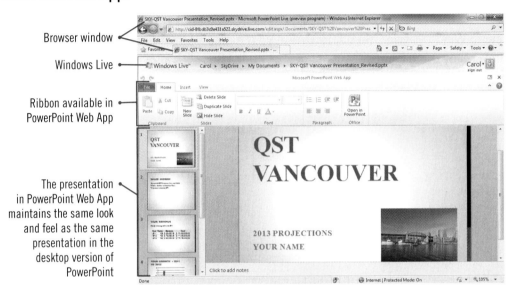

Browser window

Windows Live

Ribbon available in PowerPoint Web App

The presentation in PowerPoint Web App maintains the same look and feel as the same presentation in the desktop version of PowerPoint

You can also choose to create a new file using an Office Web App, which is saved automatically to your SkyDrive while you work. In addition, you can download a file created with an Office Web App and continue to work with the file in the full version of the corresponding Office application: Word, Excel, PowerPoint, or OneNote. Finally, you can create a Windows Live network that consists of people you want to be able to view your folders and files on your SkyDrive. You can give people permission to view and edit your files using any computer with an active Internet connection and a Web browser. Using Windows Live SkyDrive and Office Web Apps makes it easy to collaborate and share files with others.

Services available via Window Live

service	description
E-mail	Send and receive e-mail using a Hotmail account
Instant Messaging	Use Messenger to chat with friends, share photos, and play games
SkyDrive	Store files, work on files using Web Apps, and share files with people in your network
Photos	Upload and share photos with friends
People	Develop a network of friends and coworkers and use it to distribute information and stay in touch
Downloads	Access a variety of free programs available for download to a PC
Mobile Device	Access applications for a mobile device: text messaging, Hotmail, networking, and sharing photos

Get a Windows Live ID and access your SkyDrive

To work with your files online using Windows Live SkyDrive and Office Web Apps, you need a Windows Live ID. You obtain a Windows Live ID by going to the Windows Live Web site and creating a new account. Once you have a Windows Live ID, you can access your SkyDrive and then use it to store your files, create new files, and share your files with friends and coworkers.

Create a Windows Live ID

1. Open your Web browser, type windowslive.com in the Address bar, then press [Enter]. The Welcome to Windows Live page opens.

2. Click Sign up under New to Windows Live?, then click Or use your e-mail address under the Check availability button. (*Note*: If you are already using Hotmail, Messenger, or Xbox LIVE, click Sign in now.)

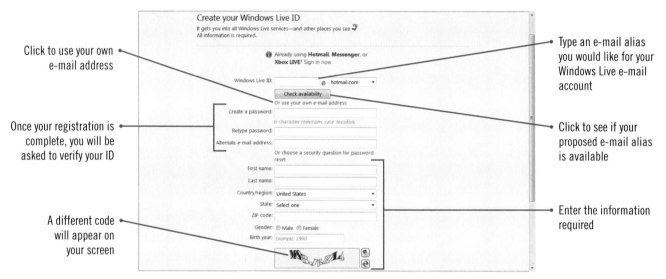

Click to use your own e-mail address

Once your registration is complete, you will be asked to verify your ID

A different code will appear on your screen

Type an e-mail alias you would like for your Windows Live e-mail account

Click to see if your proposed e-mail alias is available

Enter the information required

3. Enter the information required.

4. Enter the code as shown, then click I accept. The Windows Live home page opens. Your name appears in the upper-right corner.

Access your SkyDrive

1. On the Windows Live home page, click More, then click SkyDrive. Your SkyDrive page opens.

The current date and the weather appear here

Information about your Windows Live network

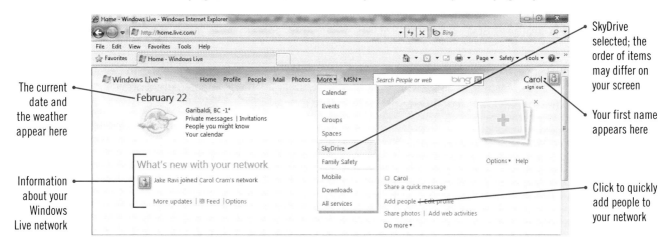

SkyDrive selected; the order of items may differ on your screen

Your first name appears here

Click to quickly add people to your network

Sign out of Windows Live

1. Click Sign Out in the upper-right corner of the Windows Live home page under your name.

Verifying your Windows Live ID

As soon as you accept the Windows Live terms, an e-mail is sent to the e-mail address you supplied when you created your Windows Live ID. Open your e-mail program, and then open the message from Microsoft with the Subject line: Confirm your e-mail address for Windows Live. Follow the simple, step-by-step instructions in the e-mail to confirm your Windows Live ID. When the confirmation is complete, you will be asked to sign in to Windows Live, using your e-mail address and password. Once signed in, you will see your Windows Live Account page.

Upload files to Windows Live SkyDrive

Once you have created your Windows Live ID, you can sign into your SkyDrive and start uploading files. You upload files to your SkyDrive so you can share the files with other people, access the files from another computer, or for additional storage. You can upload files directly to your SkyDrive from PowerPoint, Excel, Word, or OneNote.

Save a file to Windows Live SkyDrive

1. Start any Office application, then open any saved file.
2. Click the File tab, then click Save & Send. The Share tab opens. The figure below shows the PowerPoint Save & Send tab.

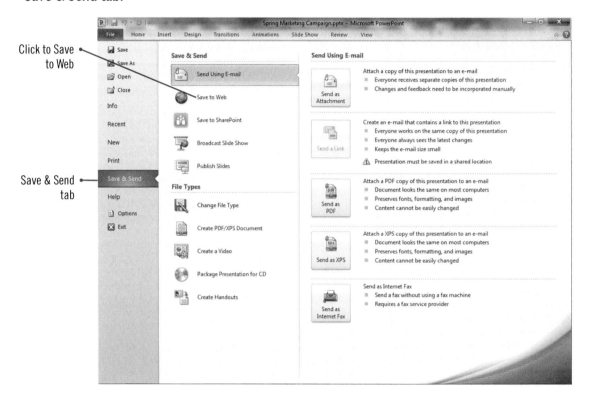

3. Click Save to Web. In a few seconds the right pane displays the folders on your SkyDrive.
4. Click the folder on your SkyDrive where you want to save the file, click Save As, wait a few seconds for the Save As dialog box to appear, then click Save. The file is saved to the folder you specified on your SkyDrive on Windows Live.

Add files to any folder on your SkyDrive

1. Open your Web browser, type windowslive.com in the address bar, then press [Enter].
2. Click More, then click SkyDrive.
3. Click the folder where you want to add a file.

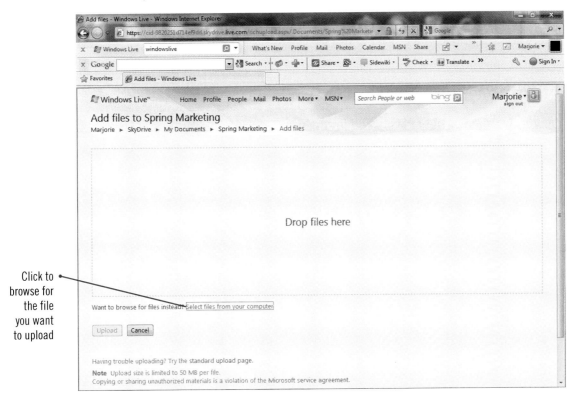

Click to browse for the file you want to upload

4. Click Select files from your computer below the Drop files here box, navigate to the folder that contains the file you want to upload, click the file to select it, then click Open.

Web Apps 2010

Work with an Office Web App

Once you have uploaded a file to SkyDrive, you can work on it using its corresponding Office Web App. **Office Web Apps** provide you with the tools you need to view documents online and to edit them right in your browser. You do not need to have Office programs installed on the computer you use to access SkyDrive and Office Web Apps. From SkyDrive, you can also open the document directly in the full Office application (for example, PowerPoint) if the application is installed on the computer you are using. As you work in a Web App, you do not have to save the file when you make changes to it; any changes are saved automatically as you work.

Edit a file on your SkyDrive using an Office Web App

1. Open your Web browser, type windowslive.com in the Address bar, then press [Enter].

2. Click More, then click SkyDrive. On your SkyDrive page, click My Documents. The My Documents page opens. The files stored on your SkyDrive appear as icons, as thumbnails, or in a detailed list.

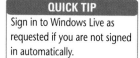

QUICK TIP
Sign in to Windows Live as requested if you are not signed in automatically.

3. Click the Office file you want to open. A new page opens with information about the file.

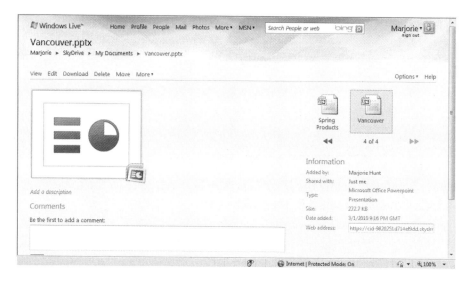

4. Click Edit. The File opens in the Office Web App. The figure on the next page shows a presentation in the PowerPoint Web App.

Browser window

URL is the file location

File path in Windows Live

Presentation in Web App maintains the same look and feel as a presentation in a desktop version of PowerPoint

Name of Web App

5. Refer to the table in this lesson to learn about the commands you can perform using the PowerPoint Web App.

tab	commands available
File	• Open in PowerPoint—Select to open the file in PowerPoint on your computer • Where's the Save Button?—When you click this option, a message appears telling you that you do not need to save your presentation when you are working in it with the PowerPoint Web App; the presentation is saved automatically as you work • Give Feedback • Close
Home	• Cut, Copy, Paste • Add a New Slide, Delete a Slide, Duplicate a Slide, and Hide a Slide • Work with text—Change the font, style, color, and size of selected text • Work with paragraphs—Add bullets and numbers, indent text, align text • Open the file in PowerPoint on your computer
Insert	• Insert a Picture • Insert a SmartArt diagram • Insert a link such as a link to another file on SkyDrive or to a Web page
View	• Editing view (the default) • Reading view • Slide Show view • Notes view

Manage files on your Windows Live SkyDrive

As you have learned, you can sign into Windows Live SkyDrive directly from the Office applications PowerPoint, Excel, Word, and OneNote, or you can access your SkyDrive directly through your Web browser. This option is useful when you are away from the computer on which you normally work or when you are using a computer that does not have Office applications installed. You can go to your SkyDrive, delete files and folders, create and organize folders, and then create or open files to work on with Office Web Apps.

Delete a file on your SkyDrive

1. Open your Web browser, type windowslive.com in the Address bar, then press [Enter]. The Windows Live homepage opens.
2. Click Sign into Windows Live, then click your e-mail address or the Sign in with a different Windows Live ID link if you do not see your e-mail address. (*Note*: Type your Windows Live ID (your e-mail) and password if prompted to do so.)
3. Click More, click SkyDrive, then click My Documents.

Current location •
Current path •
File in My Documents folder •

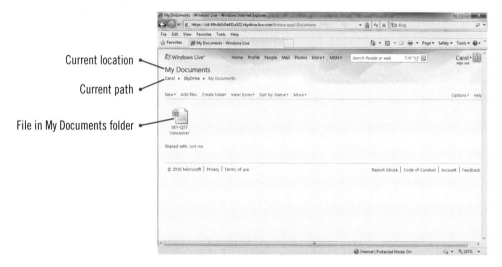

4. Click the file you want to delete, then click Delete. Click OK in the dialog box that opens. The file is removed from your SkyDrive.

Create a folder on your SkyDrive

1. On your SkyDrive page, click Create Folder.
2. Type a name for the folder you want to create.
3. Click the Share with down arrow.

4. Click the option you want to specify who can access the folder.

5. Click Next.

6. Click Select files from your computer, locate and then click the file you want to add to your new folder, then click Open. Click the Upload button. The file is added to the folder.

QUICK TIP
You can also drag files from your computer to the Drop Files Here area.

Move a file to a folder on your SkyDrive

1. Go to your SkyDrive page.

2. Open the folder that contains the file you want to move.

3. Click the file you want to move, then click Move. A list of your folders on your SkyDrive appears.

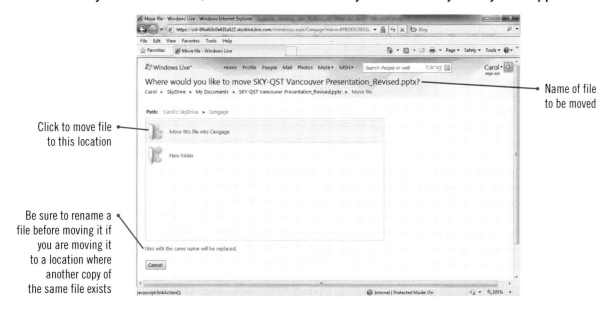

Name of file to be moved

Click to move file to this location

Be sure to rename a file before moving it if you are moving it to a location where another copy of the same file exists

4. Click the folder where you want to move the file, then click Move this file into [folder name]. The folder you specified opens and contains the file you moved into it.

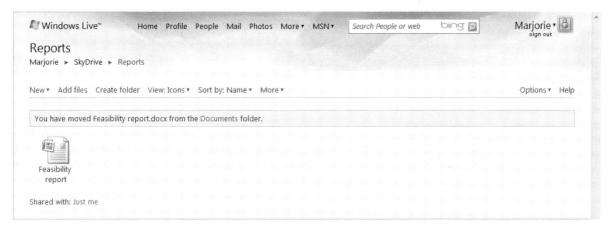

Web Apps 2010

Share files on your Windows Live SkyDrive

One of the great advantages of working with Windows Live SkyDrive is that you can share your files with others. Suppose, for example, that you want a colleague to review a presentation you created in PowerPoint and then add a new slide. You could, of course, e-mail the presentation directly to your colleague, who can then make changes and e-mail the presentation back. Alternatively, you can save time by uploading the PowerPoint file directly to your SkyDrive and then giving your colleague access to the file. Your colleague can edit the file using the PowerPoint Web App, and then you can check the updated file on your SkyDrive, also using the PowerPoint Web App. In this way, you and your colleague are working with just one version of the presentation that you both can update.

Set folder permissions on your SkyDrive

1. Open your Web browser, type windowslive.com in the Address bar, press [Enter], click More, then click SkyDrive. Your SkyDrive page opens.

2. Click the folder you want to share, click More, then click Edit permissions. The Edit permissions page opens.

QUICK TIP

Sign in to Windows Live as requested if you are not signed in automatically.

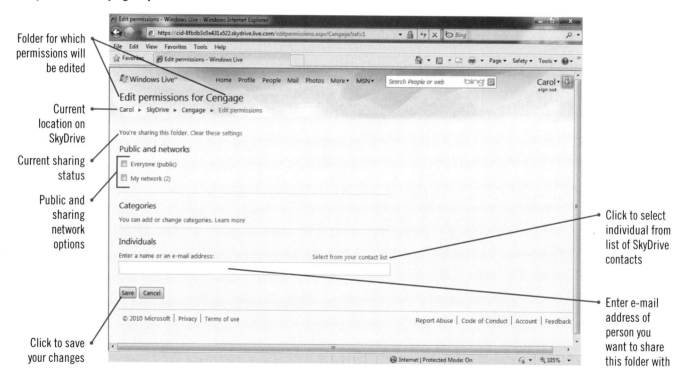

Folder for which permissions will be edited

Current location on SkyDrive

Current sharing status

Public and sharing network options

Click to save your changes

Click to select individual from list of SkyDrive contacts

Enter e-mail address of person you want to share this folder with

3. Click in the Enter a name or an e-mail address text box, then type the e-mail addresses of the people you want to share the folder with.

4. To specify the level of access each person can have to the folder, click the Can view files list arrow, then click either Can view files, or Can add, edit details and delete files.

5. Click Save. In the page that opens, you have the option of typing a message to the people you are sharing the folder with to let them know they can view the folder.

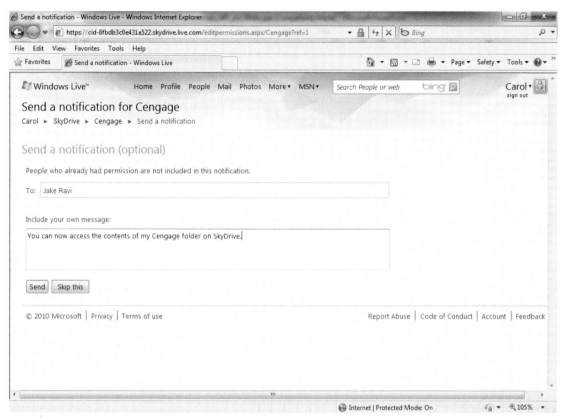

6. If you wish, click in the Include your own message text box, type a message, then click Send. (If you wish to send no message, click Skip this.)

Sharing files on your SkyDrive

When you share a folder with other people, they can open and work with your files using Office Web Apps. You can instantly see any changes they make. The people with whom you share a folder can also choose to download the file to their computers and then make changes using the full version of the corresponding Office application. Once these changes are made, each individual can then upload the file to SkyDrive and into a folder shared with you and others. In this way, you can create a network of people with whom you share your files.

Index

Note: Page numbers in boldface indicate key terms.